From
BEN-HUR
to
SISTER CARRIE

Remembering the
Lives and Works of
Five Indiana Authors

Barbara Olenyik Morrow

Guild Press of Indiana, Inc.
Indianapolis, Indiana

GUILD PRESS OF INDIANA, INC.
6000 Sunset Lane
Indianapolis, IN 46208

Library of Congress
Catalog Card Number
95-77507

ISBN 1-878208-60-8

Manufactured in the United States of America.

Text designed by Sheila Samson

CONTENTS

Acknowledgments

IN ASSEMBLING THIS BOOK I have been assisted by numerous people and institutions. I wish first to thank Judy Waanders, a librarian, bookstore owner, and book lover, who several years ago suggested to me the idea for a book about Indiana authors. Her suggestion sent me to libraries, where I—a transplanted Hoosier—began reading the novels, poems, short stories, and nonfiction works by Hoosiers deemed important in Indiana's literary history. As I delved deeper into my research, I came to rely heavily on the works of writers such as Richard Lingeman, Robert and Katharine Morsberger, and James Woodress, whose scholarship and lucid prose helped guide me in my understanding of some of Indiana's most prominent authors.

This project led me to become acquainted with numerous librarians, and I wish to thank the staffs of the Library of Congress, the New Mexico State Records Center and Archives, the Indiana Division of the Indiana State Library; the William Henry Smith Memorial Library of the Indiana Historical Society; the Lilly Library of Indiana University; the Allen County Public Library in Fort Wayne; the Warsaw Community Public Library; and my hometown library—the Eckhart Public Library in Auburn. In addition, Rose Bryan of the Geneva Public Library offered me special assistance. And Catherine Gibson, coordinator of adult services at the Indianapolis-Marion County Public Library, was exceptionally helpful.

I also wish to express my gratitude to Joann Spragg, museum coordinator and historian at the General Lew Wallace Study in Crawfordsville; Margie Sweeney, curator, and Martha Swartzlander, assistant curator, at the Gene Stratton-Porter Historic Site in Rome City; Becky Smith, curator at the Limberlost State Historic Site in Geneva; Jon

D. Kindred, field director with the James Whitcomb Riley Memorial Association in Indianapolis; Ruth Williamson, head hostess at the Riley Home in Greenfield; Marylee Hagan, director of the Vigo County Historical Society; and David G. MacLean of Decatur, a publisher and bookseller with extensive knowledge about the life and works of Gene Stratton-Porter.

I am indebted as well to J. Kent Calder, managing editor of the Indiana Historical Society's popular magazine *Traces of Indiana and Midwestern History*, for his editorial input, particularly with regard to the chapter on Theodore Dreiser. Anne Shenefield Dowd of Newport News, Virginia, also assisted me with the Dreiser chapter by supplying information about her father, Dr. Hale T. Shenefield, and providing the photograph of Dreiser at the Shenefield's wedding. I also wish to thank the estate of Theodore Dreiser for allowing me to reproduce the jacket art of the 1932 Modern Library edition of *Sister Carrie* on the cover of this book.

I greatly value the time I spent talking with Susanah Mayberry of Indianapolis, a grandniece of Booth Tarkington and author of *My Amiable Uncle*, who generously shared both stories and photographs of her famous uncle with me.

Special thanks must be given, too, to Ken Brunswick of Bryant, Indiana, for giving me a tour of the Limberlost region and for preparing the Limberlost map which appears in the Gene Stratton-Porter chapter. I am also indebted to Marla Freeman of Bryant for compiling the descriptive references from Gene Stratton-Porter's books which I used in conjunction with Brunswick's map.

Numerous people also assisted me in securing photographs for this book. I wish to thank Kathy Lendech, manager of the Clips and Stills Library of Turner Entertainment Company in Los Angeles, for providing me with photographs from the 1925 and 1959 versions of the motion picture *Ben-Hur*. Paul Saavedra, of the New Mexico State Records Center and Archives, helped me acquire the photograph of Billy the Kid. Susan Sutton, coordinator of visual reference services for the William Henry Smith Memorial Library of the Indiana Historical Society, helped me secure the photograph of James Whitcomb Riley which appears at the end of the Riley chapter. That rare photograph was taken by Mary Lyon Taylor, an Indianapolis "pictorialist" who gained much local—and some national—fame at the turn of the century with her impressionistic portraits of city residents.

A special thanks also goes to Susan Miller of Crawfordsville, who provided the Ben-Hur memorabilia which appears in a photograph in the Lew Wallace chapter. I am indebted as well to a northeastern Indiana resident who gave me the rare photographs of Gene Stratton-Porter feeding birds on a California beach. The resident prefers to remain unnamed.

I would be remiss if I failed to mention John Martin Smith of Auburn, a noted local historian who lent me books by Indiana authors and who continually offered his support. Richard Nuttall of Cathedral High School in Indianapolis was kind enough to read the entire manuscript and give encouragement. Julia Nixon, a former children's librarian and now a teacher in Kendallville, served as the final proofreader—a thankless job that she performed with expert skill. And thanks to my publisher Nancy Baxter, and to Sheila Samson, my editor, for her unstinting labor, perceptive advice, and generous help in preparing this manuscript for publication.

Finally, a heartfelt thanks goes to my husband Douglas, who patiently endured my long visits to libraries and campouts in front of the word processor, and to my four sons—Matthew, Jimmy, Andrew, and Nathan—who are as delighted as I am to have this project finished.

Barbara Olenyik Morrow
Auburn, Indiana
August 1995

PROLOGUE

AT THE TURN of the century, five years before he enthralled readers with the romantic thriller *The House of a Thousand Candles*, Meredith Nicholson, born and raised in Crawfordsville, Indiana, attempted to describe the literature and culture of his native state. In *The Hoosiers* Nicholson wrote that there was a time in Indiana when it was difficult to predict who might next get the idea in his head that he or she was a writer or poet. Nicholson noted that an Indianapolis journalist reported that there had appeared throughout the community "a peculiar crooking of the right elbow and a furtive sliding of the hand into the left inside pocket, which was unfailing preliminary to the reading of a poem."

The period Nicholson wrote about in his examination of the Hoosier state, approximately 1880 to 1920, became known as the Golden Age of Indiana Literature, a time in which Indiana authors achieved both national prominence and popular acclaim. The success Hoosier writers enjoyed prompted humorist Frank McKinney "Kin" Hubbard, creator of the cracker-barrel philosopher Abe Martin, to declare that everyone in the state "is either a politician or writer. Of course there's a fair sprinkling of tradesmen an' farmers, but only enough t' supply the wants of the writers and politicians."

Indiana authors provided readers with writing which emphasized traditional values and for a time offered shelter from the changes in society brought about by such forces as industrialization and the growth of cities. It was a time, according to former Indiana Historical Bureau Director Howard Peckham, when those living in the state developed "a sense of their own typicalness, a feeling that here was an area of real Americans." They took immense pride in what Hoosier authors produced: the local-color poetry of James Whitcomb Riley; the historical romances of Lew Wallace,

Maurice Thompson, and Charles Major; the humor of George Ade and Kin Hubbard; the fantasy of George Barr McCutcheon; the nature writing of Gene Stratton-Porter; and the mild realism of Booth Tarkington and Meredith Nicholson.

Whatever their style, many of the works that flowed from the pens of Indiana writers proved to be popular not only with the folks back home, but also with readers across the country. A 1947 study by John H. Moriarty, a Purdue University librarian, found that Hoosier authors ranked second to New Yorkers in the number of best-sellers produced in the previous forty years.

The Bobbs-Merrill Company, an Indianapolis firm, published many of these authors' works. The firm released such Indiana classics as Charles Major's *When Knighthood Was in Flower*, Maurice Thompson's *Alice of Old Vincennes*, and James Whitcomb Riley's first book of poems, *"The Old Swimmin'-Hole," and 'Leven More Poems*. By 1915 Bobbs-Merrill had produced twenty-six titles which made the annual lists of top ten best-sellers, a mark surpassing any other publisher in the country during this period.

Numerous literary organizations also sprang up to minister to those afflicted with the writing bug: the Indianapolis Literary Club in 1877, the Terre Haute Literary Club in 1881, the Ouiatenon Club (Crawfordsville) in 1883, and the Western Association of Writers (dubbed the "Literary Gravel Pit Association" by its critics) in 1886.

But the Golden Age of Indiana literature began to fade as changes in America's economic and social order accelerated after World War I. Traditional values, simple pleasures, nostalgia, and romance were less important to a postwar society preoccupied with business prosperity and such technological marvels as the automobile, radio, and motion pictures.

Today the splendor that was the Golden Age has been tarnished. If literary critics pay any attention at all to the Hoosier writers of this era they do so primarily to ridicule them as provincial and corny. Ironically, the work of an Indiana writer who seemed most out of place with other Hoosier writers of the period now meets with the greatest critical approval: Theodore Dreiser, whose childhood experiences of want and deprivation in various Indiana locations provided the foundation of his best works—*Sister Carrie*, *Jennie Gerhardt*, and *An American Tragedy*.

Those golden days may be gone, but the creative spark that inspired the Indiana authors of old lives on. Through the years Hoosiers such as Kurt Vonnegut (in *God Bless You, Mr. Rosewater*), Dan Wakefield (in *Going All the Way*), Jean Shepherd (in *In God We Trust, All Others Pay Cash*), and Michael Martone (in *Fort Wayne is Seventh on Hitler's List*) have all been influenced and shaped by their experiences in the nineteenth state.

Barbara Olenyik Morrow's work here is a reminder that, as someone once observed, Hoosiers have always been "a scribbling and a forthcoming people." In this book Morrow focuses on five "scribblers" who, through their writing, touched the lives of countless Americans—Lew Wallace, James Whitcomb Riley, Gene Stratton-Porter, Booth Tarkington, and Theodore Dreiser. These Indiana authors, each in his or her own way, made an impact on the times in which they lived. Their lives and works still offer valuable lessons for today's Hoosiers.

Ray Boomhower
Public Relations Coordinator
Indiana Historical Society

Lew Wallace

1

LEW WALLACE

I N 1959 MOVIEGOERS packed theaters to see the blockbuster *Ben-Hur*. One of the most successful movies ever made, *Ben-Hur* offered three and a half hours of thrilling entertainment, including a breathtaking chariot race in which horses collided, chariots crashed, and tense drivers lashed their teams onward with whips.

At the box office, *Ben-Hur* earned millions of dollars. It also collected awards from around the world. One film group after another called it the year's best motion picture. And at the Academy Awards ceremony in 1960, it set a record by winning eleven Oscars, with the best actor award going to Charlton Heston for his commanding performance in the title role as the handsome Jewish prince Judah Ben-Hur.

Today the movie continues to entertain new generations of viewers, especially since it has been re-released on video. But what many people don't realize is that the movie is based on a best-selling novel completed in 1880 by Lew Wallace, a Hoosier whose life was almost as exciting and dramatic as the epic film itself.

A man of action who thrived on new challenges, Wallace was at various times in his life a lawyer, soldier, politician, territorial governor, diplomat, lecturer, and author. His passion for adventure led him to become closely involved in the major events of the nineteenth century, including two wars and the taming of the American West. Likewise, his fascination with faraway places led him to travel. Twice he went to Mexico, once to help drive the French army from that country. He also journeyed to New Mexico, where he helped subdue outlaws and Apaches. He even spent four years looking after American interests in Turkey, where he toured ornate palaces, enjoyed the exotic scenery, and earned the admiration of the wealthy sultan. Everywhere he went and in everything he did, he came to know people of power and influence.

Had he chosen to record the drama of his own century, Wallace no doubt would have had important stories to tell. But his love of pageantry and derring-do, of mystery and mighty deeds, led him to write tales set in medieval and ancient times—times when, in his mind at least, men were braver, battles were more spectacular, and life offered more opportunities for glory. In reality, of course, life was rarely as picturesque and men were seldom as good or bad as portrayed by him in his fictional stories. Still, Wallace couldn't resist writing historical romances. And nineteenth-century Americans, eager for excitement and an escape from real-life problems, booed at the villains and cheered for the heroes in his elaborately plotted novels.

The most popular of those novels was *Ben-Hur*, more widely read in its time than perhaps any book except the Bible. With *Ben-Hur*, Wallace achieved the fame and fortune he had spent most of his life seeking. And through the book he hoped his memory would be kept alive: "I am looking to you and *Ben-Hur*," he wrote to his wife Susan in 1887, "to keep me unforgotten after the end of life."

* * *

When Lew Wallace was born on April 10, 1827, Indiana itself was young, having become a state only eleven years earlier. Indians still roamed the forests around the northern lake lands.

But their numbers were no match for the newly arriving wagon-loads of white settlers, who eagerly established farms and communities across the Hoosier wilderness.

Lew's birthplace was Brookville, then a thriving village in southeast Indiana. His father, David Wallace, was a graduate of the military academy at West Point and a lawyer. His mother, Esther French Test, was the daughter of a judge and congressman. Esther died in July 1834, when Lew and his two brothers were still quite young, and a few years later David married nineteen-year-old Zerelda Sanders of Indianapolis. Lew was uncomfortable around his stepmother at first and, as he recalled years later, was "sulky and stubborn" in her presence. But when he ran off to the woods for two days and then returned seriously ill with "the croup," Zerelda stayed by his sickbed, nursing him back to health. After that, their relationship bloomed. Years later, when Wallace sketched Ben-Hur's mother as being strong and loving, he admitted to having Zerelda in mind.

In the summer of 1832, when Lew was five, the Wallaces moved across the state to Covington, a small town on the Wabash River near Illinois. Five years later David Wallace, who was active in politics, was elected Indiana's sixth governor, and the Wallaces moved to Indianapolis, the new Hoosier capital. Founded only seventeen years earlier, Indianapolis in 1837 was—in Lew's words—"scarcely emerged from the woods." Its streets were little more than country roads; one or more cows grazed outside each home. Still, everywhere young Lew looked there were signs of growth—of land being cleared of timber, of railroad tracks being laid, of canals being dug. Lew was especially impressed with the freshly stuccoed State House, grander than anything he had ever before seen.

The library in the State House became one of Lew's favorite places to visit. There he went about "prospecting the shelves," using a stepladder to help him locate all the illustrated books in the collection. There, too, he became acquainted with the works of American novelists, especially James Fenimore Cooper, whose romantic style of storytelling would later influence Wallace's own writing. "My name was Idleness," Wallace said of himself years later, "except that I read—every moment that I was still I was reading."

When he wasn't sitting still, he was usually exploring nearby fields, creeks, and forests. "When I was a boy," he once wrote, "I ran wild in the great woods of my native State. I hunted, fished, went alone, slept with my dog, was happy, and came out with a constitution [good health]." He especially loved summer, for that's when he ran wild from sunrise to sunset without shoes or coat. Autumn, too, was a favorite season as he joined birds and chipmunks in gathering wild fruits and nuts. "Who better than I," he recalled, "knew where to look for the fattest hazel and hickory nuts, chincapins the least acrid, grapes in largest cluster, pawpaws the most melting?"

From time to time Lew attended school, but he never liked the classroom. He hated even more the schoolmasters who thrashed him for not concentrating on his studies. The beatings were often bloody and left welts on his legs. Still, no matter how severe the punishment, the boy's restless spirit could not be tamed. To a friendly farmer, who regularly asked Lew if he had been flogged by a certain schoolmaster, the boy always replied: "Yes, but he didn't make me holler."

Not all Lew's schoolmasters were quick to use the rod. In 1840, when Lew was thirteen, he attended a church-run school taught by a patient and understanding professor named Samuel K. Hoshour. To encourage the boy's interest in reading and writing, Hoshour lent him books and advised his young pupil to read about the birth of Jesus in the Bible, something Lew had never done. Fascinated by St. Matthew's Gospel account of the wise men, Lew began asking himself questions that he would continue to ask for years: *Who were those wise men from the East? How many were there? How did they know to follow the star?*

"Little did I dream then," Wallace wrote much later, "what those few verses were to bring me—that out of them *Ben-Hur* was one day to be evoked."

Now when Jesus was born in Bethlehem of Judea in the days of Herod the king, behold, wise men from the East came to Jerusalem, saying, "Where is he who has been born king of the Jews? For we have seen his star in the East, and have come to worship him."

   . . . and lo, the star which they had seen in the East went before them, till it came to rest over the place where the child was. When they saw the star, they rejoiced exceedingly with great joy; and going into the house they saw the child with Mary his mother, and they fell down and worshiped him. Then, opening their treasures, they offered him gifts, gold and frankincense and myrrh.

                    —The Holy Bible
                    The Gospel of Matthew,
                    Chapter 2

* * *

In the early spring of 1846, tensions were mounting between the United States and Mexico. The governments of both countries disagreed on where to draw the boundaries for Texas, which had recently joined the Union as the twenty-eighth state.

Wallace was not yet twenty years old. He was living in Indianapolis, studying law in his father's office, and working late into the night on a newly begun project—a novel. A few years earlier he had read a historical account of the conquest of Mexico in the 1500s by the Spanish invader Hernando Cortes. Wallace instantly developed a special interest in the subject and decided to write his own adventure tale, focusing on the drama between Cortes and the Aztec ruler

Montezuma. He wrote strictly for his own pleasure and at his own pace. Publication wasn't a goal.

But just as Mexico's history fascinated Wallace, he was even more intrigued by the prospect of the United States declaring war against its southern neighbor. "The uncertainty was more than interesting—it plunged me into a fever of excitement," he recalled. "I wanted the war, thinking of little else, and I went about hunting news and debating the probabilities."

In May 1846, after fighting broke out between Mexican troops and American soldiers near the Rio Grande, Congress officially declared war against Mexico. The youthful Wallace opened a recruiting office in Indianapolis and within three days he had signed up enough volunteers to form a company, which elected him second lieutenant. Hungry for war, he couldn't wait to march south—to the land of wide pastures and palmettos, to the long-ago fighting ground of Cortes and Montezuma.

"Had I not been reading about [war] all my life?" he wrote later. "And had not all I had read about it wrought in me that battle was the climax of the sublime and terrible, and that without at least one experience of the kind no life could be perfect?"

In July Wallace and the First Regiment Indiana Volunteers sailed by steamboat to New Orleans and then by clipper ship to Mexico. But instead of being assigned inland near the battlefront, they were ordered to guard a deserted beach. There soldiers sweltered in the humidity, suffered from mosquito and chigger bites, and became ill from the food and water. In time, diseases such as smallpox swept the camp, killing men in such numbers that there was not enough wood for coffins. "Sickness is stalking around us day and night," Wallace wrote his brother William. "Seven were buried yesterday . . . Truly we live in the midst of death."

Though he longed to be permitted to move his troops and prayed that he himself would see battle, the orders he hoped

Courtesy Lew Wallace Study

Wallace at age nineteen.

MARY CLEMMER, a friend of Lew Wallace's who shared his romantic outlook on life, described him this way after his return from the Mexican War:

He is fashioned of the refined clay of which nature is most sparing, nearly six feet high, perfectly straight, with a fine fibered frame all nerve and muscle, and so thin he cannot weigh more than a hundred and thirty pounds. He has profuse black hair, a dark, beautiful face, correct in every line, keen, black eyes deeply set, with a glance that on occasion may cut like fine steel. Black beard and mustache conceal the firm mouth and chin. His modest, quiet manner is the only amende that can be made for being so handsome. In a crowd anywhere you would single him out as a king of men.

for never came. Instead, a year after he arrived in Mexico, he and his fellow Hoosiers were sent home, their tour of duty over, just as the war itself was drawing to a close. Much to Wallace's surprise, no cheering crowds or boisterous bands greeted the returning soldiers. The Mexican War, like the Vietnam War more than a century later, had not been popular at home, and many Americans had even accused the United States government of stirring up trouble along the border.

Wallace, however, continued to believe the United States had acted justly in driving the Mexicans back from the disputed land, part of which today is New Mexico—a territory over which he would later become governor. Wallace also clung to his romantic notions about war. He had seen soldiers live under wretched conditions. He had observed commanding officers act incompetently. And he had witnessed "quarreling, fighting, slandering, court-martialling, etc." among the troops. But he still believed it was noble to serve in the military, and he still thought of war as a grand drama, full of flying flags, beating drums, and gallant young men prepared to defend their country's honor.

"I have never regretted," Wallace wrote later, "the year left behind me as a soldier in Mexico."

* * *

On April 12, 1861, nearly fourteen years after Wallace returned from Mexico, Confederate soldiers fired on Fort Sumter in the harbor outside Charleston, South Carolina. Those shots signalled the start of America's long and bloody Civil War.

Wallace knew that for practical reasons he should resist the urge to put on a military uniform. At age thirty-four he was no longer young. He also had a family to attend to; in 1852 he had married Susan Elston, and a year later their son Henry was born. In addition, Wallace's law practice in Crawfordsville

needed his attention, as did his political career. Since returning from Mexico, Wallace had twice been elected prosecuting
attorney, and in 1856 he had been elected to the state senate
as a Democrat.

Still, even though it made sense for Wallace to excuse himself from military service, he could not. When Indiana Governor Oliver P. Morton asked him to find men to serve in the
Union Army, he quickly recruited nearly twice the number
of volunteers requested. He also was promoted to colonel and
given command of the Eleventh Indiana Regiment of Volunteers. He had no doubt, as he later wrote in his autobiography, that "the conflict would be long and great." But the prospect of riding into battle, seated confidently atop his horse,
sword drawn at the sound of trumpets, excited him. And he
was certain that the war "would also be crowded with opportunities for distinction," opportunities he felt he had been
cheated out of during the Mexican War.

Within the first ten months of the war Wallace—handsome, erect, and a dashing figure in his showy uniform—
proved to be an able commander. Under his leadership, the
Eleventh Indiana drove Confederate soldiers from a town in
Virginia in June 1861, a raid which President Lincoln himself praised. Eight months later, in February 1862, Wallace
helped direct the Union forces which captured Fort Henry and
Fort Donelson, two important Confederate strongholds in
western Tennessee. "I never heard music as fascinating and
grand as that of battle," Wallace wrote his wife Susan after
the victory at Fort Donelson. He was rewarded with a pro-
motion to major general, the youngest person to hold that
rank in the Union Army.

But as promising as his military career seemed in March
of 1862, all was to change in April near the Tennessee-Mis-
sissippi border. There, at the Battle of Shiloh, Wallace suffered a setback from which he never recovered.

On the morning of April 6, 1862, Confederate soldiers attacked the Union Army camped near Shiloh Church, just west

of the Tennessee River. Wallace was commanding troops nearby and received orders from Major General Ulysses S. Grant to proceed to the battlefield. Somehow a misunderstanding occurred and Wallace, instead of moving his men as Grant had wanted, marched in the wrong direction and missed the first day's battle. His blunder was costly. Grant had desperately needed Wallace's troops, and by nightfall the Union Army was on the verge of collapse.

Wallace and his men were present for the second day's fighting. They, along with other newly arrived troops, joined Union soldiers in pushing the Confederates from the smoldering battlefield. But as the rebel forces retreated, the Union Army had little to cheer about. Thousands of soldiers lay slaughtered on the ground. Next to them lay thousands more of the wounded and the dying. In all, more Confederate and Union soldiers were killed or injured during those two days of intense fighting than the total number of Americans who died or were wounded in the Revolution, the War of 1812, and the Mexican War combined.

Not surprisingly, the public was shocked and horrified when it learned of the bloodbath at Shiloh. Newspapers in the North criticized Grant for not being better prepared. So did politicians and even some of his own troops. But Grant, resenting the attacks and feeling compelled to defend himself, argued that Wallace—by arriving late—was to blame for the Union Army's near defeat on the first day. Wallace, hoping to set the record straight, insisted that Grant's unclear orders were responsible for his delay.

Historians have long been divided as to who was at fault. Wallace was never officially punished. But he was relieved of his command, and newspapers, having attacked Grant at length, soon switched to picking on Wallace. Frustrated, Wallace spent the summer of 1862 at his home in Crawfordsville, waiting for further orders. Eventually he was given other assignments for which he was duly commended. His daring stand at the Battle of Monocacy in July 1864 earned him widespread praise. There he delayed the march of rebel soldiers on Washington, D.C., thus saving the capital from disaster.

But unlike Grant, who eventually became commander of the entire Union Army and a national hero, Wallace had to settle at the war's end for far less glory. Even Hoosiers, who recognized him as the state's most distinguished Civil War soldier, could not forget his role at Shiloh. "Shiloh and its slanders!" Wallace complained to his wife more than twenty years later. "Will the world ever acquit me of them?" And in 1900, nearly forty years after Shiloh, a still-bitter Wallace said to a fellow soldier: "O, the lies, the lies that were told to make me the scapegoat to bear off the criminal mistakes of others . . . Think of what I suffered."

* * *

Wallace never enjoyed practicing law. "It was a drag," he once said. "I worried at it, and it worried me." But he had a family to provide for and bills to pay. After the Civil War, he resumed his law career.

He didn't reopen his law practice immediately, however. With the assassination of President Lincoln at Ford's Theater in April 1865, a military commission was organized to try the eight prisoners accused of participating in the murder plot. Partly because of his legal training, Wallace was appointed to serve on the commission. In May, while the nation was still mourning Lincoln's death, the commission began hearing evidence in what was then the most dramatic trial in American history. By June Wallace and the other commission members had found all eight defendants guilty, with four of them sentenced to death by hanging.

After the Lincoln trial, Wallace found yet another excuse to avoid his law practice. Napoleon III of France, eager to extend his empire into the New World, had a year earlier installed a government in Mexico led by the Archduke

Ferdinand Maximilian. The Mexican people, led by their president Benito Juarez, were trying to drive out the French army and turned to the United States for help.

Always eager for adventure and believing that France had no right to be in Mexico, Wallace began recruiting American soldiers in the fall of 1865 to aid Juarez's troops. The following summer he even traveled to Mexico, spending seven months there trying to deliver much-needed military supplies and weapons. He never saw battle, and although he had expected the Mexican government to pay him handsomely, he received no money—at least initially—for his efforts. Eventually, Napoleon III ordered his troops back to France, Maximilian was killed by Juarez's army, and democracy returned to Mexico. Wallace, deeply in debt, returned to Crawfordsville in February 1867. With no ideas as to how else he could earn money, he reopened his law office.

In his spare time, he resumed work on his novel about Mexico which he had begun twenty-five years earlier. Though his writing had been interrupted many times over the years, he had managed to keep composing his story, jotting down ideas and sentences "at way-stations, of evenings here and there, in breaks of business . . ." He wrote in the style of authors he had admired in his youth, "romantics" such as James Fenimore Cooper and the Scottish novelist Sir Walter Scott. Like them, he avoided writing about life as it often was—uneventful, tiresome, and frustrating. Instead, he loaded his epic tale with heroic characters in dazzling costumes, set amid scenes of splendor. And into his plot, which was based on the conflict between the Aztec Indians and the invading Spaniards, he wove suspense, savagery, superstition, pageantry, and love.

In the spring of 1872, when he finally finished his manuscript titled *The Fair God*, Wallace decided to submit it to a publisher in Boston. The editor of that firm quickly responded that Wallace's work was "fresh and fascinating. " By August 1873, *The Fair God* was in bookstores.

The public liked the novel—more than seven thousand copies were sold the first year—but critics were divided. Some praised it as a "remarkable" work of historical fiction and among "the worthiest of modern romances." Others, who preferred the "realism" evident in new novels such as Edward Eggleston's *The Hoosier School-Master*, faulted Wallace for his excessive romanticism—for overdoing the drama and sketching scenes too majestically. "There is spirit in the book," wrote one reviewer, "but it is the spirit of a theatrical spectacle rather than a work of art . . ."

Back in Crawfordsville, not everyone was impressed with Wallace's literary success. Many Hoosiers regarded writers as idlers who wasted time with pen and paper when they should have been planting corn or feeding livestock. Wallace soon found himself the butt of jokes and sarcastic remarks from local townsfolk. And his literary reputation almost ruined his law practice: "As soon as the jury of farmers and village merchants heard the word 'novel' they uttered hearty guffaws," Wallace said years later. "I might as well have appeared in court dressed as a circus clown."

Still, the ridicule didn't discourage the lawyer-turned-writer. Wallace soon began work on a second novel set in an even more distant land, the Middle East, in an even more distant time in history—around the birth of Christ. The book would take seven years to complete and require painstaking research. But it would bring Wallace what he had never achieved on a battlefield: worldwide recognition and wealth.

* * *

In the early 1870s, when he began writing *Ben-Hur*, Wallace was neither a regular churchgoer nor devoutly religious. "I had no convictions about God or Christ," he recalled years later. "I neither believed nor disbelieved in them. The preachers had made no impression on me." What had made a lasting impression, however, was the story of the wise men in St. Matthew's Gospel. "Far back as my memory goes of things read by or to me," he said, "those lines took a hold on my imagination beyond every other passage of Scripture."

Not long after *The Fair God* was published, Wallace decided to write about the three wise men in a way which would allow readers to relive their sighting of the star, their ride through the desert, their meeting with King Herod, and their presenting of gifts to the Christ child. Wallace had hoped to sell the story to a magazine. But after finishing it, he laid it aside and began working on another tale about a Jewish nobleman named Judah Ben-Hur and his once-best friend, a Roman commander named Messala. That story was well under way when Wallace met Colonel Robert G. Ingersoll.

Ingersoll, a Civil War veteran who had fought at Shiloh, was well known in the late 1800s for his controversial lectures in which he criticized the Bible and Christianity. In the fall of 1876 Wallace spent an evening aboard a train with Ingersoll, and during that visit he became painfully aware of his own "ignorance" regarding religious matters. That very night he decided he would begin studying the Bible and the life of Christ.

Wallace was reluctant, however, to give up his writing. He hadn't forgotten his story about the wise men, and it suddenly occurred to him that perhaps that manuscript could serve as the beginning of a more ambitious project—a novel about Christ, ending with his death on the cross.

"I had my opening; it was the birth of Christ," Wallace recounted years later. "Could anything be more beautiful? As a mere story, the imagination of man has conceived nothing more crowded with poetry, mystery . . . nothing sweeter with human interest." And as for a final scene, "as a climax or catastrophe to be written up to . . . what could be more stupendous than the Crucifixion?"

But though he had an opening and a conclusion for a novel, Wallace wondered how he would fill the middle, especially since the Bible says nothing about Jesus' life from the time he was a young boy until he began his ministry. After several weeks of reflection, Wallace decided to "use the blank to show the religious and political condition of the world" at the time Christ lived. Wallace's other unfinished story, about the two former friends, was already set in ancient times. Why not, Wallace asked himself, link Ben-Hur's story with that of Christ's. That way he could tell readers what it was like to live in Palestine under Roman rule in the first century, and, as he noted, "perhaps those conditions would demonstrate a necessity for a Savior."

Long fascinated with the ancient world, Wallace was determined to portray it accurately. His research led him to the Library of Congress in Washington, D. C., where he read book after book relating to the Jews. He also studied Roman history, examined maps of the Holy Land, and pored over reference books to learn about Middle Eastern customs and costumes. Whenever possible, he talked to travelers who told Wallace about the birds, animals, and plants in the region.

"I had never been to the Holy Land," he wrote later. "In making it the location of my story, it was needful not merely to be familiar with its history and geography, I must be able to paint it, water, land, and sky, in actual colors . . . Ponder the task! . . . I had to be so painstaking!"

But as much as Wallace enjoyed writing *Ben-Hur*, he was unable to give the project his complete attention. In August 1878 President Rutherford B. Hayes offered him a job as governor of New Mexico, then still a territory. Lured by the promise of more adventure, Wallace accepted the appointment, and for the next three years he devoted himself to bringing outlaws to justice and protecting white settlers from angry Apaches. Still, the adventures of Ben-Hur were never far from his mind. Late at night, after he had finished his official duties, he escaped to a dungeon-like room in the back of the rambling, one-story adobe building that served as the governor's palace in Santa Fe. There, sitting at a rough pine table and working by lamplight, he wrote the final chapters of *Ben-Hur*.

There, too, he began recopying the entire manuscript in purple ink.

"The ghosts, if they were ever about, did not disturb," he later wrote. And as the project drew to a close, he informed his wife Susan in January 1880, "What a long, long work it has been, a labor of love! How many hours and days and weeks it has consumed! Frightful to think of; and yet I know no happier way of passing time, none which takes me so completely out of this world . . ."

* * *

In 1893, thirteen years after Wallace's second novel was published, a survey of public libraries revealed that *Ben-Hur: A Tale of the Christ* was loaned more frequently than any other book in America.

Seven years later, in 1900, *Ben-Hur* had become the best-selling novel of the nineteenth century, outselling the enormously popular antislavery tale *Uncle Tom's Cabin.* And in 1980, one hundred years after *Ben-Hur* was published, it could still claim this distinction: it had never been out of print.

"I would rather be the author of *Ben-Hur*," a Lafayette, Indiana man wrote to Wallace in 1886, voicing the enthusiasm so many Americans had for the book, "than to be the President of the United States."

Wallace had no idea in 1880, when he submitted his manuscript to a New York publisher, that the book would be such a smashing success. He knew that many churchgoing people objected to novels of any kind, on the grounds that it was sinful to read anything that wasn't true. He also knew that making Christ a character in a novel, as he had done, had the potential of offending readers. Nineteenth-century Americans were accustomed to reading about Christ in the Bible and in nonfiction books. But many Americans believed that portraying Christ in *fiction* would be irreverent, even blasphemous.

Sensitive to how the public might react, Wallace composed his story with great care. He made every effort to show respect for Christ and Christianity. He also wisely centered the story's action around the proud Ben-Hur, who—after surviving three years as a galley slave and plotting revenge against his former friend Messala—in time came to accept Jesus as Christ. Wallace's careful treatment of his material paid off; many Americans whose religious views had in the past led them to shun novels found *Ben-Hur* to be exciting and inspiring reading. And clergymen were among the loudest praise-singers.

"Few books that I have read have given me greater pleasure and I thoroughly appreciate the high and noble purpose which has evidently directed its composition," the Anglican bishop of Portsmouth, England, wrote Wallace. Declaring *Ben-Hur* to be "the object of my glowing sympathy and unbounded admiration," a Roman Catholic priest in Wisconsin gushed, "The Messiah appears before us as I always wished him depicted to men."

The novel's religious theme wasn't all that appealed to readers, however. As in *The Fair God*, Wallace spiced *Ben-Hur* with romance, daring acts of heroism, and thrilling action scenes involving battling warships and racing chariots. He also filled the chapters with hordes of fascinating characters—pirates, gladiators, lepers, a deal-making sheik, slaves chained to their oars in Roman galleys. For an untold number of Americans in the late nineteenth century, ancient history came alive within the pages of *Ben-Hur*. And even though critics complained that Wallace should have written a more realistic novel set in modern times, readers didn't care. To them, the saga of Ben-Hur was, in the words of one critic, "like cold water to a thirsty soul."

By the end of the 1800s, fans of *Ben-Hur* were urging Wallace to rewrite the story as a play. Wallace hesitated, fearing that it would be difficult to preserve the "religious atmosphere" on stage. Eventually, however, he gave his permission to a theatrical company to write and produce a stage version, complete with real camels and chariots being pulled by galloping horses on treadmills. The play opened on Broadway in late 1899 to an enthusiastic audience. And for the next twenty-one years millions of people, including many church-goers who had never before entered a theater, paid to see it in New York and in cities around the world. Special trains were even chartered to transport people from small towns and rural areas to communities where the play was touring. And in many towns, people looked forward to the arrival of *Ben-Hur*'s cast with as much or even more excitement than they did the circus.

Movie producers took note of *Ben-Hur*'s success on stage. In 1925, during the silent-screen era of movies, the film studio of Metro-Goldwyn-Mayer released the first film version of *Ben-Hur*, a lavish production that critics praised and audiences loved. Thirty-four years later, MGM released an even more spectacular version of the film—with sound, on wide screen, and in color. That 1959 film starring Charlton Heston was a box-office success around the world and remained so for many years. In 1971, when it appeared on American television for the first time, it was watched by more people than any movie previously shown on TV.

Wallace died before seeing all that his novel gave birth to in the twentieth century. But even in 1899, when shown the sets for the stage version of *Ben-Hur*, he couldn't help but shake his head in wonderment.

"My God!" he said at the time. "Did I set all this in motion?"

* * *

When *Ben-Hur* was published in 1880, Wallace was fifty-three, old enough to begin thinking about retirement. But slowing down was out of the question for him. For the next twenty-five years, until his death in 1905, he remained a man

The chariot race from the 1959 motion picture *Ben-Hur*.

THROUGH sixty years every American within reach of print and pictures, and many a foreigner, must at least have heard of *Ben-Hur*; most came to know it and remember it; thousands upon thousands read the book, saw the play, enacted it themselves. They were thrilled, frightened, delighted, amused, disgusted, bored—and almost without exception they cherished the chariot race until their dying day.

—Irving McKee, author of *"Ben-Hur" Wallace*

Photo by Bob Luse

THERE WAS a time when the name Ben-Hur seemed to be everywhere in America. Texas, Virginia, and Arkansas named towns Ben-Hur. Businesses marketed Ben-Hur products—toys, candy, spices, cigars, baking powder. A Ben-Hur rose was developed; a Ben-Hur bicycle was manufactured. Amusement parks and county fairs featured Ben-Hur carousels.

Today the name isn't used for commercial purposes nearly as much as it once was. But it hasn't disappeared from the landscape or from our conversations. As Robert and Katharine Morsberger noted in their book *Lew Wallace: Militant Romantic*: "Ben-Hur has had a lasting and pervasive influence on American culture and mores . . . Like Sherlock Holmes and Tarzan, Ben-Hur has entered the language and become a part of our common culture."

on the go—a man for whom "going was life."

Upon finishing his gubernatorial duties in New Mexico, Wallace set sail in 1881 for Turkey, where he served as an American diplomat responsible for protecting U.S. citizens and looking after trade rights. His residence was in Constantinople, the capital of the once-powerful Ottoman Empire and a city which intrigued him as few other places had. There he admired magnificent palaces, world-famous mosques, and beautiful churches. He explored noisy bazaars where merchants sold cigarettes, silks, and carpets. And he marveled at the city's fascinating collection of people, which included Turks, Africans, Armenians, Greeks, Persians, and Europeans. He stayed four years in that foreign port, during which time he became friends with the empire's ruler, Abdul Hamid II. When Wallace's assignment ended, the sultan urged him to stay and accept a post with the Turkish government. Uninterested, Wallace sailed for home in 1885.

Back in Crawfordsville, the still-vigorous Wallace found much to keep him busy. He wrote a lengthy poem based on a Turkish legend. He tinkered with a play he had begun nearly two decades earlier and began work on his autobiography. He also completed his third novel, *The Prince of India,* a tale of intrigue set in Constantinople during the fifteenth century. The public, expecting another *Ben-Hur*, was sorely disappointed with the book, which was published in 1893. *The Prince of India*'s slow opening caused many readers to give up before reading even half of it. And literary critics faulted Wallace for churning out more of the same—historical fiction loaded with too much flowery language and far too much romanticism.

When not researching and writing, Wallace lectured extensively; his fame from *Ben-Hur* made him a popular speaker. In his spare time, he designed and directed the construction of a large study next to his Crawfordsville home, a place he called the "pleasure-house for my soul." He also retained his longtime interest in politics and military affairs.

When the Spanish-American War began in 1898, Wallace, still filled with romantic notions about battle, volunteered to command a brigade of black soldiers from Indiana. For a while it appeared as if he might be offered a commission. But the offer never came, apparently because of his age: he was seventy-one.

It wasn't until the last year of his life, when he began suffering from stomach cancer, that Wallace had to limit his activities. He knew he was dying, and upon learning of the death of an old friend he wrote, "He is but a day's march ahead of us; we will overtake him soon." By late 1904 he spent most of his time in his study, resting on a couch, eating little. He died at his home on February 15, 1905, surrounded by his family.

In announcing his death, the Crawfordsville newspaper wrote, "His mind was clear to the last. He fought the good fight and died, as he had lived, without fear." Hoosiers everywhere took note of the news, with the flag at the State House lowered to half mast. Admirers by the hundreds filed past his body, which lay in state in his study. One of Indiana's most prominent citizens, James Whitcomb Riley, honored his memory with a poem.

After his death, *The Indianapolis News* proposed that his statue be erected in the Capitol in Washington, D.C. The Indiana legislature eventually approved the idea, and in 1910 a statue of Wallace was unveiled in Statuary Hall in the Capitol building. Each state was entitled to have two of its citizens honored. Of all the distinguished Americans depicted in statue there, Wallace is the only novelist.

To those who knew Wallace and knew of him, he was an extraordinary man. As the Hoosier novelist Booth Tarkington noted, a "moral grandeur" surrounded him and he belonged to "men of action who are men of brain and heart besides." He lived at a time when many Americans tried to leave their mark on a nation still growing to maturity, and Wallace—hearty, energetic, optimistic—never tired of trying to serve his country or of playing a prominent role in public affairs. Few Hoosiers of the nineteenth century were as involved as he was in so many varied aspects of "public" life.

As eagerly as Wallace sought real-life adventures, however, he also dreamed about imaginary adventures, many of which he put into his novels. He took special pleasure in writing his action-packed tales, and as he noted to his wife Susan in his later years:

> I have tried many things in the course of the drama— the law, soldiering, politics, authorship, and, lastly, diplomacy—and if I may pass judgment upon the success achieved in each, it seems now that when I sit down finally in the old man's gown and slippers, helping the cat to keep the fireplace warm, I shall look back upon *Ben-Hur* as my best performance.

SUGGESTIONS FOR FURTHER READING

McKee, Irving. *"Ben-Hur" Wallace: The Life of General Lew Wallace*. Berkeley: University of California Press, 1947.

Morsberger, Robert E. and Katharine. *Lew Wallace: Militant Romantic*. New York: McGraw-Hill, 1980.

Wallace, Lew. *An Autobiography*. 2 vols. New York: Harper & Brothers, 1906. (Wallace recorded his life through the Civil War; his wife and Mary Hannah Krout completed the writing.)

Ben-Hur

(From Book Fifth, Chapter xiv, The Race)

When the dash for position began, Ben-Hur, as we have seen, was on the extreme left of the six. For a moment, like the others, he was half blinded by the light in the arena; yet he managed to catch sight of his antagonists and divine their purpose. At Messala, who was more than an antagonist to him, he gave one searching look. The air of passionless hauteur characteristic of the fine patrician face was there as of old, and so was the Italian beauty, which the helmet rather increased; but more—it may have been a jealous fancy, or the effect of the brassy shadow in which the features were at the moment cast, still the Israelite thought he saw the soul of the man as through a glass, darkly: cruel, cunning, desperate; not so excited as determined—a soul in a tension of watchfulness and fierce resolve.

In a time not longer than was required to turn to his four again, Ben-Hur felt his own resolution harden to a like temper. At whatever cost, at all hazards, he would humble this enemy!

Prize, friends, wagers, honor—everything that can be thought of as a possible interest in the race was lost in the one deliberate purpose. Regard for life even should not hold him back. Yet there was no passion, on his part; no blinding rush of heated blood from heart to brain, and back again; no impulse to fling himself upon Fortune: he did not believe in Fortune; far otherwise. He had his plan, and, confiding in himself, he settled to the task, never more observant, never more capable. The air about him seemed aglow with a renewed and perfect transparency.

When not half-way across the arena, he saw that Messala's rush would, if there was no collision, and the rope fell, give him the wall; that the rope would fall, he ceased as soon to doubt; and, further, it came to him, a sudden flash-like insight, that Messala knew it was to be let drop at the last moment (prearrangement with the editor could safely reach that point in the contest); and it suggested, what more Roman-like than for the official to lend himself to a countryman who, besides being so popular, had also so much at stake? There could be no other accounting for the confidence with which Messala pushed his four forward the instant his competitors were prudentially checking their fours in front of the obstruction—no other except madness.

It is one thing to see a necessity and another to act upon it. Ben-Hur yielded the wall for the time.

The rope fell, and all the fours but his sprang into the course under urgency of voice and lash. He drew head to the right, and, with all the speed of his Arabs, darted across the trails of his opponents, the angle of movement being such as to lose the least time and gain the greatest possible advance. So, while the spectators were shivering at the Athenian's mishap, and the Sidonian, Byzantine, and Corinthian were striving, with such skill as they possessed, to avoid involvement in the ruin, Ben-Hur swept around and took the course neck and neck with Messala, though on the outside. The marvellous skill shown in making the change thus from the extreme left across to the right without appreciable loss did not fail the sharp eyes upon the benches: the Circus seemed to rock and rock again with prolonged applause. Then Esther clasped her hands in glad surprise; then Sanballat, smiling, offered his hundred sestertii a second time without a taker; and then the Romans began to doubt, thinking Messala might have found an equal, if not a master, and that in an Israelite!

And now, racing together side by side, a narrow interval between them, the two neared the second goal.

The pedestal of the three pillars there, viewed from the west, was a stone wall in the form of a half-circle, around which the course and opposite balcony were bent in exact parallelism. Making this turn was considered in all respects the most telling test of a charioteer; it was, in fact, the very feat in which Orestes failed. As an involuntary admission of interest on the part of the spectators, a hush fell over all the Circus, so that for the first time in the race the rattle and clang of the cars plunging after the tugging steeds were distinctly heard. Then, it would seem, Messala observed Ben-Hur, and recognized him; and at once the audacity of the man flamed out in an astonishing manner.

"Down Eros, up Mars!" he shouted, whirling his lash with practised hand—"Down Eros, up Mars!" he repeated, and caught the well-doing Arabs of Ben-Hur a cut the like of which they had never known.

The blow was seen in every quarter, and the amazement was universal. The silence deepened; up on the benches behind the consul the boldest held his breath, waiting for the outcome. Only a moment thus: then, involuntarily, down from the balcony, as thunder falls, burst the indignant cry of the people.

The four sprang forward affrighted. No hand had ever been laid upon them except in love; they had been nurtured ever so tenderly; and as they grew, their confidence in man became a lesson to men beautiful to see. What should such dainty natures do under such indignity but leap as from death?

Forward they sprang as with one impulse, and forward

leaped the car. Past question, every experience is serviceable to us. Where got Ben-Hur the large hand and mighty grip which helped him now so well? Where but from the oar with which so long he fought the sea? And what was this spring of the floor under his feet to the dizzy eccentric lurch with which in the old time the trembling ship yielded to the beat of staggering billows, drunk with their power? So he kept his place, and gave the four free rein, and called to them in soothing voice, trying merely to guide them round the dangerous turn; and before the fever of the people began to abate, he had back the mastery. Nor that only: on approaching the first goal, he was again side by side with Messala, bearing with him the sympathy and admiration of every one not a Roman. So clearly was the feeling shown, so vigorous its manifestation, that Messala, with all his boldness, felt it unsafe to trifle further.

As the cars whirled round the goal, Esther caught sight of Ben-Hur's face—a little pale, a little higher raised, otherwise calm, even placid.

Immediately a man climbed on the entablature at the west end of the division-wall, and took down one of the conical wooden balls. A dolphin on the east entablature was taken down at the same time.

In like manner, the second ball and second dolphin disappeared.

And then the third ball and third dolphin.

Three rounds concluded: still Messala held the inside position; still Ben-Hur moved with him side by side; still the other competitors followed as before. The contest began to have the appearance of one of the double races which became so popular in Rome during the later Caesarian period—Messala and Ben-Hur in the first, the Corinthian, Sidonian, and Byzantine in the second. Meantime the ushers succeeded in returning the multitude to their seats, though the clamor continued to run the rounds, keeping, as it were, even pace with the rivals in the course below.

In the fifth round the Sidonian succeeded in getting a place outside Ben-Hur, but lost it directly.

The sixth round was entered upon without change of relative position.

Gradually the speed had been quickened—gradually the blood of the competitors warmed with the work. Men and beasts seemed to know alike that the final crisis was near, bringing the time for the winner to assert himself.

The interest which from the beginning had centred chiefly in the struggle between the Roman and the Jew, with an intense and general sympathy for the latter, was fast changing to anxiety on his account. On all the benches the spectators bent forward motionless, except as their faces turned following the contestants. Ilderim quitted combing his beard, and Esther forgot her fears.

"A hundred sestertii on the Jew!" cried Sanballat to the Romans under the consul's awning.

There was no reply.

"A talent—or five talents, or ten; choose ye!"

He shook his tablets at them defiantly.

"I will take thy sestertii," answered a Roman youth, preparing to write.

"Do not so," interposed a friend.

"Why?"

"Messala hath reached his utmost speed. See him lean over his chariot-rim, the reins loose as flying ribbons. Look then at the Jew."

The first one looked.

"By Hercules!" he replied, his countenance falling. "The dog throws all his weight on the bits. I see, I see! If the gods help not our friend, he will be run away with by the Israelite. No, not yet. Look! Jove with us, Jove with us!"

The cry, swelled by every Latin tongue, shook the velaria over the consul's head.

If it were true that Messala had attained his utmost speed, the effort was with effect; slowly but certainly he was beginning to forge ahead. His horses were running with their heads low down; from the balcony their bodies appeared actually to skim the earth; their nostrils showed blood-red in expansion;

LEW WALLACE   29

their eyes seemed straining in their sockets. Certainly the
good steeds were doing their best! How long could they keep
the pace? It was but the commencement of the sixth round. On
they dashed. As they neared the second goal, Ben-Hur turned
in behind the Roman's car.

The joy of the Messala faction reached its bound: they
screamed and howled, and tossed their colors; and Sanballat
filled his tablets with wagers of their tendering.

Malluch, in the lower gallery over the Gate of Triumph,
found it hard to keep his cheer. He had cherished the vague
hint dropped to him by Ben-Hur of something to happen in the
turning of the western pillars. It was the fifth round, yet the
something had not come; and he had said to himself, the sixth
will bring it; but, lo! Ben-Hur was hardly holding a place at the
tail of his enemy's car.

Over in the east end, Simonides' party held their peace.
The merchant's head was bent low. Ilderim tugged at his beard,
and dropped his brows till there was nothing of his eyes but an
occasional sparkle of light. Esther scarcely breathed. Iras alone
appeared glad.

Along the home-stretch—sixth round—Messala leading,
next him Ben-Hur, and so close it was the old story—

> *First flew Eumelus on Pheretian steeds;*
> *With those of Tros bold Diomed succeeds:*
> *Close on Eumelus' back they puff the wind,*
> *And seem just mounting on his car behind;*
> *Full on his neck he feels the sultry breeze,*
> *And, hovering o'er, their stretching shadow sees.*

Thus to the first goal, and round it. Messala, fearful of
losing his place, hugged the stony wall with perilous clasp; a
foot to the left, and he had been dashed to pieces; yet, when the
turn was finished, no man, looking at the wheel-tracks of the
two cars, could have said, here went Messala, there the Jew.
They left but one trace behind them.

As they whirled by, Esther saw Ben-Hur's face again, and it was whiter than before.

Simonides, shrewder than Esther, said to Ilderim, the moment the rivals turned into the course, "I am no judge, good sheik, if Ben-Hur be not about to execute some design. His face hath that look."

To which Ilderim answered, "Saw you how clean they were and fresh? By the splendor of God, friend, they have not been running! But now watch!"

One ball and one dolphin remained on the entablatures; and all the people drew a long breath, for the beginning of the end was at hand.

First, the Sidonian gave the scourge to his four, and, smarting with fear and pain, they dashed desperately forward, promising for a brief time to go to the front. The effort ended in promise. Next, the Byzantine and Corinthian each made the trial with like result, after which they were practically out of the race. Thereupon, with a readiness perfectly explicable, all the factions except the Romans joined hope in Ben-Hur, and openly indulged their feeling.

"Ben-Hur! Ben-Hur!" they shouted, and the blent voices of the many rolled overwhelmingly against the consular stand.

From the benches above him as he passed, the favor descended in fierce injunctions.

"Speed thee, Jew!"

"Take the wall now!"

"On! loose the Arabs! Give them rein and scourge!"

"Let him not have the turn on thee again. Now or never!"

Over the balustrade they stooped low, stretching their hands imploringly to him.

Either he did not hear, or could not do better, for half-way round the course and he was still following; at the second goal even still no change!

And now, to make the turn, Messala began to draw in his left-hand steeds, an act which necessarily slackened their speed. His spirit was high; more than one altar was richer of his vows; the Roman genius was still president. On the three pillars only six hundred feet away were fame, increase of fortune, promotions, and a triumph ineffably sweetened by hate, all in store for him! That moment Malluch, in the gallery, saw Ben-Hur lean forward over his Arabs, and give them the reins. Out flew the many-folded lash in his hand; over the backs of the startled steeds it writhed and hissed, and hissed and writhed again and again; and though it fell not, there were both sting and menace in its quick report; and as the man passed thus from quiet to resistless action his face suffused, his eyes gleaming, along the reins he seemed to flash his will; and instantly not one, but the four as one, answered with a leap that landed them alongside the Roman's car. Messala, on the perilous edge of the goal, heard, but dared not look to see what the awakening portended. From the people he received no sign. Above the noises of the race there was but one voice, and that was Ben-Hur's. In the old Aramaic, as the sheik himself, he called to the Arabs—

"On, Atair! On, Rigel! What, Antares! dost thou linger now? Good horse—oho, Aldebaran! I hear them singing in the tents. I hear the children singing and the women—singing of the stars, of Atair, Antares, Rigel, Aldebaran, victory!—and the song will never end. Well done! Home to-morrow, under the black tent—home!—On Antares! The tribe is waiting for us, and the master is waiting! 'Tis done! 'tis done! Ha, ha! We have overthrown the proud. The hand that smote us is in the dust. Ours the glory! Ha, ha!—steady! The work is done—soho! Rest!"

There had never been anything of the kind more simple; seldom anything so instantaneous.

At the moment chosen for the dash, Messala was moving in a circle round the goal. To pass him, Ben-Hur had to cross the track, and good strategy required the movement to be in a forward direction; that is, on a like circle limited to the least possible increase. The thousands on the benches understood it all: they saw the signal given—the magnificent response; the four close outside Messala's outer wheel, Ben-Hur's inner wheel behind the other's car—all this they saw. Then they heard a crash loud enough to send a thrill through the Circus, and, quicker than thought, out over the course a spray of shining white and yellow flinders flew. Down on its right side toppled the bed of the Roman's chariot. There was a rebound as of the axle hitting the hard earth; another and another; then the car went to pieces; and Messala, entangled in the reins, pitched forward headlong.

To increase the horror of the sight by making death certain, the Sidonian, who had the wall next behind, could not stop or turn out. Into the wreck full speed he drove; then over the Roman, and into the latter's four, all mad with fear. Presently, out of the turmoil, the fighting of horses, the resound of blows, the murky cloud of dust and sand, he crawled, in time to see the Corinthian and Byzantine go on down the course after Ben-Hur, who had not been an instant delayed.

The people arose, and leaped upon the benches, and shouted and screamed. Those who looked that way caught glimpses of Messala, now under the trampling of the fours, now under the abandoned cars. He was still; they thought him dead; but far the greater number followed Ben-Hur in his career. They had not seen the cunning touch of the reins by which, turning a little to the left, he caught Messala's wheel with the iron-shod point of his axle, and crushed it; but they had seen the transformation of the man, and themselves felt the heat and glow of his spirit, the heroic resolution, the maddening energy of action with which, by look, word, and gesture, he so suddenly inspired his Arabs. And such running! It was rather the long leaping of lions in harness; but for the lumbering chariot, it seemed the four were flying. When the Byzantine and Corinthian were half-way down the course, Ben-Hur turned the first goal.

And the race was WON!

The consul arose; the people shouted themselves hoarse; the editor came down from his seat, and crowned the victors.

The fortunate man among the boxers was a low-browed, yellow-haired Saxon, of such brutalized face as to attract a second look from Ben-Hur, who recognized a teacher with whom he himself had been a favorite at Rome. From him the young

Jew looked up and beheld Simonides and his party on the balcony. They waved their hands to him. Esther kept her seat; but Iras arose, and gave him a smile and a wave of her fan—favors not the less intoxicating to him because we know, O reader, they would have fallen to Messala had he been the victor.

The procession was then formed, and, midst the shouting of the multitude which had had its will, passed out of the Gate of Triumph.

And the day was over.

Photo by Bob Luse

Wallace's study in Crawfordsville.

IN 1896, WORKERS BEGAN constructing a study next to Lew Wallace's home in Crawfordsville—a building that one newspaper called "the most beautiful author's studio in the world . . . a dream of oriental beauty and luxury."

Wallace had long yearned for a place where he could "write, and . . . think of nothing else." As early as 1885 he had confided in a letter to his wife that "I want to bury myself in a den of books. I want to saturate myself with the elements of which they are made and breathe their atmosphere until I am of it."

The study that Wallace eventually designed was a blend of architecture—Roman, Greek, Byzantine. Requiring three years to build, it featured a forty-foot-high tower copied from a church in Italy, a copper dome and skylight reminiscent of the mosques Wallace had seen in Turkey, and an entrance gate designed from an eleventh-century abbey in France. Characters from Wallace's novels were carved in limestone along the top of the outside walls.

In 1977 the study and three and a half acres of grounds were declared a National Historic Landmark by the federal government. Today the study is maintained by the city of Crawfordsville as a museum, where many relics from Wallace's career are on display. Among the featured items are a Confederate flag captured during the Battle of Monocacy, the arms and shield of an Apache warrior killed while Wallace was governor of the New Mexico Territory, and a Roman soldier's costume used in the 1959 movie *Ben-Hur*.

Wallace was able to enjoy his beloved study for only a few years before his death in 1905. But he savored his time in what for him was "a pleasure-house for my soul."

WHILE SERVING AS GOVERNOR of the New Mexico Territory, Lew Wallace had dealings with an outlaw who has since become a legend in America—the notorious "Billy the Kid."

The Kid, whose real name was William H. Bonney, witnessed the murder of a man in Lincoln County, New Mexico, in 1879. Wallace, who as governor was trying to bring law and order to the county, wanted Bonney to testify as to what he saw. But Bonney, who had already killed several men himself, was trying to escape capture from a gang of outlaws who didn't want him to be a court witness.

Determined to find Bonney, Wallace offered a thousand-dollar reward for his arrest. To Wallace's surprise, he soon received a letter from the Kid, who said he would talk to Wallace if the governor would promise not to punish him for his earlier crimes and offer him protection. A secret meeting was arranged. Bonney showed up, and he and Wallace struck a deal. Several weeks later, at what was then the most sensational trial in New Mexico's history, Bonney told a jury about the murder of Huston Chapman, the man he had seen gunned down.

After the trial Bonney turned more and more to crime. Wallace, still working to reduce violence and lawlessness in New Mexico, posted a five-hundred-dollar reward for the Kid's arrest, and a sheriff named Pat Garrett eventually captured the young desperado. From his jail cell, Bonney wrote Wallace again, demanding that the governor honor his earlier promise to help him avoid standing trial on old murder charges. But this time Wallace didn't respond to Bonney's letters. He believed that the outlaw was no longer entitled to special treatment. Since the Chapman trial, Bonney had murdered another man, and his gang of cattle rustlers and horse thieves had terrorized the county.

In July 1881, two and a half months after Bonney had escaped from jail, Sheriff Garrett tracked the twenty-one-year-old fugitive to a house where he was hiding and shot him dead. Almost immediately, the crimes committed and daring exploits performed by Bonney gave rise to legend. And today, as that legend is retold, Lew Wallace's name continues to be associated with it.

Warrant for Billy the Kid's death, signed by Wallace.

Billy the Kid.

Courtesy Lew Wallace Study

Courtesy Lew Wallace Study

(Left) Major General Wallace at age thirty-four. (Right) Wallace in his early fifties, while governor of the New Mexico Territory and around the time he completed *Ben-Hur.*

Pencil sketch by Wallace of El Palacio, Santa Fe, where he completed *Ben-Hur.* The sketch became an engraving for Susan Wallace's book *The Land of the Pueblos.*

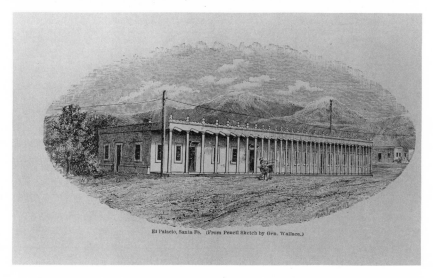

El Palacio, Santa Fe. (From Pencil Sketch by Gen. Wallace.)

Three generations of Wallaces—grandson Lew Jr., Wallace, and son Henry.

Susan Elston Wallace, his wife.

Wallace smoking a long-stemmed pipe at his fishing camp on the Kankakee River.

A sketch of the treadmill that was built for the Broadway stage production of *Ben-Hur* around 1899.

Wallace with three friends, including James Whitcomb Riley (seated in the middle), around 1900.

Ramon Novarro (right) as Ben-Hur and Francis X. Bushman as Messala in the 1925 film version of *Ben-Hur*.

Charlton Heston (right) as Ben-Hur and Stephen Boyd as Messala in the 1959 motion picture.

James Whitcomb Riley

2

JAMES WHITCOMB RILEY

T HE NINETEENTH-CENTURY humorist Mark Twain thought James Whitcomb Riley was one of the funniest storytellers and best poetry readers in America. The famous British writer Rudyard Kipling was so impressed with Riley's rhymes about childhood that he composed a poem titled "To J.W.R." The respected *Christian Science Monitor* compared Riley to Abraham Lincoln, declaring that both had a "sincere love" of people. And President Woodrow Wilson, in honor of Riley's sixty-sixth birthday in 1915, offered his tribute of "affectionate appreciation . . . for the many pleasures [Riley] has given me, along with the rest of the great body of readers of English."

Few American poets have been as loved or as celebrated as James Whitcomb Riley was during his lifetime. Known as "The Hoosier Poet," he was in reality the "people's poet," a man whose poems were recited in homes and schoolhouses across the nation. Even Americans who disliked poetry confessed to enjoying his work. As the writer Hamlin Garland noted in 1896: "He is read by people who never before read poetry in their lives."

Riley helped his popularity by being a superb entertainer. In an age when there was no radio, television, or motion pictures, Americans often attended performances that featured poetry readings. Exceedingly skilled at reciting his verses, Riley could make audiences laugh until their sides hurt or reduce them to tears. "His reading is, in reality, fine acting," a writer for the *Philadelphia Telegram* commented in 1899. "Not since the time of [Charles] Dickens has there been an author who possessed in so great a measure the talent Mr. Riley displays."

Of the more than one thousand poems Riley wrote, most were about common things in life—juicy pies and fragrant coffee at "Old Aunt Mary's," bullfrogs and lightnin'-bugs on the "banks o' Deer Crick," a sun-soaked sky on a day "knee-deep in June." Riley's poems also affirmed the values of common people: their commitment to family, their attachment to farms and small towns, their respect for nature.

Beyond that, Riley wrote in a language—actually, two languages—that common people could understand. He composed many of his verses in "correct" or standard English. Yet unlike other writers of his era, who copied the poets of early nineteenth-century England, he carefully avoided using old-fashioned words and phrases such as "Thou'rt" and "er'st." When not using standard English, Riley wrote in dialect, the plain and unpolished speech of country people in Indiana, as in

> *O the Raggedy Man! He works fer Pa;*
> *An' he's the goodest man ever you saw!*

Today the dialect verses remain among the best-remembered of Riley's poems. But whatever language he used, his meaning was always clear. "Riley speaks our tongue," Indiana Senator Albert Beveridge declared in 1905. "He voices the sentiment and wisdom of the common man . . . He is the interpreter of the common heart."

Beloved as he was throughout the nation, Riley was especially adored and revered in Indiana. His statue was erected in his hometown of Greenfield. Indiana schools, parks, and a children's hospital in Indianapolis were named after him, as were restaurants, highways, and canned goods. Even a passenger train that used to cross the state daily between Cincinnati and Chicago was called "The James Whitcomb Riley." In the 1930s, when the Indiana State Library was built, Riley's name was carved in marble in the main reference room, alongside the names of the world's leading poets.

Today Hoosiers still speak affectionately about Riley, whose life has become something of a legend in the state. His family "homestead" in Greenfield and his Lockerbie Street home in Indianapolis attract thousands of visitors each year. And his birthday, at one time observed in classrooms across the nation, is still celebrated by many schoolchildren around Indiana.

Riley's literary reputation, however, has suffered with the years. Modern critics judge most of Riley's poems to be mediocre and even bad; they fault the Hoosier poet for being more interested in writing verses which sold well than in producing literature of lasting importance. Still, even the critics admit that few poets ever captured the public's attention the way Riley did. And they credit him with preserving, especially in his dialect poems, the spirit of frontier and village life at the very moment it was disappearing in America.

"Riley recorded life in the Middle West, in a rural community, in the decade immediately preceding the Civil War, and historians might do well to consult his work," bibliographer Dorothy Russo noted in 1944. "Out of his poetry there emerges a pattern of people, scenes and customs that rings true . . . Because of all these things it is possible that his work will live on in the hearts of generations to come."

* * *

Greenfield, the government seat of Hancock County, Indiana, was a village of about three hundred people in the

As a child, Riley had corn-silk hair and freckles, which he once tried to rub off with a solution advertised as a "Positive cure for freckles." Much to Riley's dismay and embarrassment, the solution never produced the intended results and instead briefly turned his face "yellow as an Easter egg!"

Years later, he described in rhyme how he appeared as boy:

> *My hair was just white as a dandelion ball,*
> *My face freckled worse than an old kitchen wall.*

1840s. It consisted of log cabins and framed cottages surrounded by woods thick with beech, ash, and walnut trees.
Through the center of town ran a dirt highway known as the
National Road, the main route across the Allegheny Mountains to the western frontier. Over that busy thoroughfare
traveled a steady parade of pioneers—in oxcarts and "prairie schooners," in pack trains and on foot. When gold was
discovered in California in the late 1840s, westward-bound
adventurers streamed through Greenfield, some stopping long
enough to spend the night, others pausing only briefly to rest
their horses and buy supplies.

It was into this Hoosier community, in a small cabin alongside the National Road, that James Whitcomb Riley was born
on October 7, 1849. His parents, Reuben and Elizabeth Riley,
named him after James Whitcomb, one of Indiana's early
governors.

James' parents were well-liked and respected by Greenfield's residents. Slender and blue-eyed, Elizabeth Riley was
known for her patience, pleasant singing voice, and knack for
composing rhymes, which occasionally were printed in the
county newspaper. Reuben Riley was good at giving speeches
and was often called upon to speak at barbecues and rallies.
Active in politics, Reuben was Greenfield's first mayor, and
before that he had represented Hancock County in the state
legislature. A successful attorney, Reuben was able to provide comfortably for his family, and in 1852 the Rileys moved
from their log cabin into a two-story home along the National
Road, the same home that operates today as a museum in
Riley's honor.

James, or "Jim" as he was known to his friends, was small
compared to other boys his age and not very strong or skilled
at rough sports. But he loved to play outdoors, and he was
especially drawn to the fields and woods just outside Greenfield, where he walked barefoot down dusty lanes, splashed
in "cricks," hunted for watermelons in cornfields, and climbed

mulberry trees. Years later, the Hoosier countryside of Riley's boyhood would come alive in his poems about the "old swimmin'-hole" in Brandywine Creek, checkerboard-farms where "the frost is on the punkin and the fodder's in the shock," and fragrant orchards where

> *Mr. Bluejay, full o' sass,*
> *In them baseball clothes o' his,*
> *Sportin' round the orchard jes'*
> *Like he owned the premises!*

An imaginative boy, Jim also found ways to amuse himself indoors, especially when an orphan named Mary Alice Smith came to live briefly with the family. Mary Alice earned her keep by washing the dishes, shooing the chickens off the porch, and doing other chores around the house. When her work was done, she would sit in the kitchen and, as the flickering candlelight cast eerie shadows on the walls, tell Jim spooky "witch-tales." Years later, Mary Alice appeared in one of Riley's most popular poems as "Little Orphant Annie." Still enjoyed by young people today, the poem features an orphan who has "come to our house to stay" and who warns naughty children to be good or else

> *the Gobble-uns'll git you*
> *Ef you*
> *Don't*
> *Watch*
> *Out!*

When Jim was eleven his father left home to serve as a captain in the Civil War. Money was scarce, and Elizabeth had to be resourceful in order to care for Jim and his four brothers and sisters. But food was plentiful, and the family

POEMS SUCH AS "Little Orphant Annie" eventually earned Riley the title of "children's poet." The title seemed to fit, given that he often wrote about young people and about the delights and heartaches of childhood. But Riley, who never had any children, didn't deliberately try to appeal to youngsters. Rather, his poems were intended for adults who clung to tender memories of their youth—just as he treasured memories of his boyhood in Greenfield. Riley was willing to let other poets ponder the problems of the world and comment on life's mysteries. He much preferred to take adults back in time—to innocent, carefree days when they sailed through the air on that "old swing in the lane," played with "the squirt-gun uncle maked me," fed beechnuts and "chinkypins" to pet coons, and marveled at the Raggedy Man who knew all about

> *Giunts, an' Griffuns, an' Elves,*
> *An' the Squidgicum-Squees 'at swallers ther'selves!*

"We were in heaven when we were children but we did not know it," Riley once said. "Restore the rapture and rhythm of my childhood days and I cannot think of many improvements."

managed to get by. Jim helped where he could with the war effort—by greeting soldiers at the train depot and filling their canteens with milk, running errands for women making bandages, and assisting with programs to benefit the Soldier's Aid Society. In his free time, he began reading fiction and poetry recommended by an English immigrant who owned a shoeshop in Greenfield. Among his favorite authors were the American poet Henry Wadsworth Longfellow and the British novelist Charles Dickens, whose warm and humorous tales about the poor and helpless in London greatly moved Jim and later influenced his sketches of ordinary Hoosiers.

When the war was finally over in 1865, Reuben returned home. His arm was partially paralyzed as a result of a battle injury, and he could not hear well. He tried to revive his law practice, which he had left to a nephew. But clients were few, and Reuben, faced with a mounting stack of bills, was eventually forced to sell the "Old Homestead."

"We were poor," Jim would write years later, "so poor we had to move into a cheerless house in the edge of a cornfield, our homestead having been lost . . . ."

Though he was glad when his father returned home, Jim—by then a teenager—sensed a growing gap between Reuben's interests and his own. Practical and matter-of-fact, Reuben wanted his son to prepare for a career in law. Softhearted and dreamy, Jim enjoyed drawing, writing rhymes, playing the fiddle, acting in local dramas, and entertaining people with his wit. He had no desire to be an attorney, and he hated schoolwork with a passion. He failed so miserably at arithmetic that, in his words, "half the town pitied me." And history lessons were pure torture because "dates melted out of my memory as speedily as tin-foil on a red-hot stove."

In 1870, after having spent much of his teen years playing hookey and even dropping out of school for a while, Jim tried one more time to graduate. He earned passable, even good, grades at a new school in Greenfield, signalling to Reuben that perhaps his twenty-year-old fun-loving son was finally maturing. But after one "term," Jim had had enough of the classroom. He quit, never to come back.

"My school life," he later said, "was a farce all the way through." And on another occasion, he added: "Omit the schoolroom from my history entirely, and the record of my career would not be seriously affected."

> *I see, across the schoolroom floor,*
> *The shadow of the open door,*
> *And dancing dust and sunshine blent*
> *Slanting the way the morning went,*
> *And beckoning my thoughts afar*
> *Where reeds and running waters are . . .*

> —"The All-Golden," 1883

* * *

In August 1870 Elizabeth Riley died suddenly. Jim had been especially close to his mother, and his grief over her death was so great that an older brother, John Andrew, wrote in his diary, "What shall we do with Jim now that mother is dead?"

Reuben was himself at loose ends over what to do with his son. He arranged for Jim to work with a local sign painter, in hopes that he would at least learn a trade. Jim proved to be skilled with a paintbrush, and within a year he opened his own shop and was painting advertisements on barns and fences throughout Hancock County. But he barely earned a living and remained restless. In May 1872, when "Doc" McCrillus' medicine wagon rolled into Greenfield, Jim sensed an opportunity for adventure, and he convinced the white-whiskered McCrillus to give him a job.

McCrillus, like many "medicine salesmen" in the late 1800s, traveled around in a brightly painted wagon and tried to entice local merchants and townsfolk to buy specially concocted "remedies" to cure their aches and pains. Jim's job was to paint signs advertising Doc's "Standard Remedies." He also helped entertain curious farmers and villagers who gathered around the back steps of the wagon, where Doc conducted business. Jim would sing, play a borrowed guitar, and do funny imitations of people. He'd also recite stories, including "The Bear Story," a tale that Jim's brother Alex composed as a young boy and which Jim revised into an enormous crowd-pleaser.

"I laughed all the time," Jim later said, recalling his vaga-bond days with McCrillus. "Miles and miles of somber land-scapes were made bright with merry song and when the sun shone and all the golden summer lay spread out before me, it was glorious. I drifted on through it like a wisp of thistledown, careless of how, or when, or where the wind should anchor me."

But as carefree and enjoyable as that gypsy life was, Jim needed to find more permanent work. At summer's end, he left McCrillus' show and began painting signs across north-ern Indiana, eventually adding partners and calling his busi-ness The Graphic Company. In his spare time he practiced writing verses and jingles. He also began giving entertain-ing lectures in churches and schoolhouses at which he "tried out" his poems and other stories. Turnout was small at first, leaving Jim discouraged. But he persisted, adding new pieces to his program, revising others, and carefully noting how his body movements—the tilt of his head, the arch of his eye-brows—helped captivate listeners. His efforts began to pay off. He started developing a reputation, especially around Indianapolis, as a popular speaker.

Still, Jim remained a young man adrift, without steady work or a permanent home. When he acquired money—as he did when he joined another medicine show, the Wizard Oil Company—he quickly spent it. When his money ran out, he suffered. More than once he had to skimp on meals and take lodging in "little rat-trap" hotels, and even then he couldn't always pay his bills. On at least one occasion, while living in Marion, Indiana, he was so cold that he was forced to line his bedcovers with newspapers. On another occasion, he tried to trade his sleeve buttons for a railroad ticket.

"I was floundering," Jim would later write of those years. A disappointed Reuben could only agree.

* * *

In April 1877, at the age of twenty-seven, James Whitcomb Riley finally landed a job that paid a regular salary. He was hired to edit a weekly newspaper in Anderson, Indiana, and he quickly impressed readers by spicing dull copy with his own dash of humor. Within four weeks the *Anderson Democrat*'s circulation doubled. His salary was raised from forty to sixty dollars a month.

In September, however, Riley was fired from the *Democrat* for playing a practical joke. With the help of some friends, he wrote and published in a Kokomo, Indiana, newspaper a poem identified as a long-lost work by Edgar Allan Poe, a famous American poet dead for many years. The hoax was inspired by Riley's frustration with newspaper and magazine editors in the East. Throughout the 1870s they had been rejecting poems he sent them—rejections he believed were based on the fact he wasn't a well-known or "established" writer. He was convinced that "no matter the little worth of a poem, if a great author's name was attached, it would be certain of success and popularity." He devised the "Poe" ruse to prove his point, although unfortunately for Riley, his hoax succeeded—all too well.

Newspapers from New York to San Francisco reprinted the poem, launching a literary discussion nationwide as to whether Poe was really the author. Eventually Riley confessed to what he called a "boyish prank." But newspaper editors and literary critics weren't amused, and Riley was widely denounced as an "unscrupulous young man" who had committed a "great fraud." Shamefaced and disheartened, he returned to Greenfield. "It was," he later recalled, "the most dismal period of my life."

Humiliated as he was, however, Riley actually benefited from all the publicity. When he resumed giving humorous programs, he discovered that his name was well-known around the state, and he began drawing bigger and more enthusiastic crowds. Weekly newspapers also began showing a greater interest in publishing his work. Eventually the *Indianapolis Journal*, to which he had been a regular contributor, asked him to join the staff full-time. In November 1879 Riley moved to Indianapolis, rented a room in a boarding house, and became the *Journal*'s "resident poet," the man to whom editors looked for light verse and occasional sketches in prose.

While at the *Journal* Riley began to seriously experiment with poems written in "dialect." Since childhood, he had paid close attention to how people talked. He had also shown a special talent for mimicking the conversations of others, especially the odd assortment of travelers who journeyed through Greenfield on the National Road. He never lost his "ear" for language, and he increasingly felt an urge to write as country folk in Indiana actually spoke, rather than to record their speech in proper English.

Beginning in June 1882, the *Journal* published a series of Riley verses in dialect, which included "When the Frost Is on the Punkin," one of his most famous poems. Written from the viewpoint of an Indiana farmer named Benjamin F. Johnson, the poems created an immediate sensation in the state. By the following summer, they were published in book form as *"The Old Swimmin'-Hole," and 'Leven More Poems*, and they continued to be talked about and widely read. Admirers of Riley's work in dialect included prominent writers such as Mark Twain and Joel Chandler Harris.

The dialect poems were successful partly because they

were full of cheer, optimism, and humor. They were written at a time of rapid change in America, as families left their farms and moved to cities to work in factories. Many people were confused by or uneasy with the changes, and Riley's poems offered them, temporarily at least, an escape from their worries and fears. While reading his verses, Americans were transported to the quiet towns and cozy villages of their youth—where "wortermelons" grew fat on the vine, where the "wimmern-folks" made mince and apple-butter, where fiddlers used to "plonk and plunk and plink," and where everyone felt safe and needed.

The dialect poems also appealed to readers because they were fresh. With their loose and easy rhythms and homespun phrases, they were not an imitation of the verses of English writers. As the author and statesman John Hay noted, after reading a copy of *"The Old Swimmin'-Hole,"* the dialect poems had "a distinct and most agreeable flavor, which is entirely their own." The respected writer Hamlin Garland agreed, saying, "I found the verses . . . utterly unlike any other I had read."

Riley was thrilled to have finally found his "voice" as a poet, and during the next twenty-five years he would write hundreds of verses in dialect. He never completely abandoned "correct" English; some of his most popular poems, such as "Away" and "The Name of Old Glory," were composed using proper grammar and diction. But Riley's great fame would come from recording the simple and natural speech of country people. And from his dialect verses would come his most memorable characters—The Raggedy Man, Little Orphant Annie, Doc Sifers, 'Lizabuth-Ann, Tradin' Joe, Uncle Sidney, and others. Ultimately, Riley's work in dialect would be his major—and lasting—contribution to American literature.

When the frost is on the punkin and the fodder's in the shock,

And you hear the kyouck and gobble of the struttin'
  turkey-cock,
And the clackin' of the guineys, and the cluckin' of the
  hens,
And the rooster's hallylooyer as he tiptoes on the fence;
O, it's then's the times a feller is a-feelin' at his best,
With the risin' sun to greet him from a night of peaceful
  rest,
As he leaves the house, bareheaded, and goes out to feed
  the stock,
When the frost is on the punkin and the fodder's in the
  shock.

* * *

While working for the *Indianapolis Journal*, Riley continued to travel around Indiana, reciting his poetry and telling stories. As his reputation as a poet and entertainer grew, a Boston-based company arranged for him to give lectures, and soon Riley was impressing out-of-state audiences with his wit and charm just as he had earlier delighted Hoosiers.

When he appeared on stage, Riley was not the rustic poet in rumpled overalls and straw hat, with hayseed behind the ears, that some city dwellers expected. Rather, he was always elegantly dressed in evening clothes, his face clean-shaven, his blond hair carefully brushed. A modest man, he had a habit of speaking haltingly at first, in a way that aroused the curiosity of his listeners. After that, it was his custom to remove the glasses perched atop his nose and to begin his readings, using carefully designed gestures, expressions, and shadings of his voice. As if by magic, the audience soon had the distinct impression it was listening not to Riley, but to the characters in his poems and stories—to an old man recalling his "sweetheart" in sunbonnet and checkered dress, to a wide-eyed boy chasing a bear, to a little orphaned girl, to a humble Hoosier farmhand.

RILEY WAS very serious about his work in dialect. Insisting that what he wrote was an accurate recording of how Hoosier farmers and villagers spoke in the mid-1800s, he refused to permit anyone to tamper with his poems. He forbade editors to replace ungrammatical phrases with proper English. Neither would he allow them to change his unusual spelling of words to a "correct" form. In his poems words such as "been" appeared as "ben," "ought" appeared as "ort" and "did you ever" appeared as "jevver"—to name just a few. As Riley once noted in a letter to a friend, "One 'get' for 'git' would prove fatal to me."

As popular as Riley's dialect poems were, not everyone in Indiana appreciated them. Some people complained that Riley used Hoosier dialect to poke fun at farmers and small-town folk. Others insisted that he actually invented the dialect. He was accused of creating words and phrases that he thought sounded good and that suited his own literary purposes.

Even if Riley took some liberties with Hoosier speech, it was never his intent to ridicule or put down the people of his home state. He was deeply attached to Indiana, and his poems were written to let others, especially Easterners, know something about the interests and customs of Midwesterners. In addition, Riley never said he was recording the speech of his contemporaries. Rather, he was preserving the speech of an earlier era—the speech he had heard in his youth before the Civil War. As times changed, and as Hoosiers became better educated, the folk language of the state began to change. The Hoosier poet, as Riley's biographer Marcus Dickey noted, was determined to rescue "from oblivion . . . the thought of an age in Indiana that was fast passing away."

"So vivid were his impersonations and so readily did he communicate the sense of atmosphere, that one seemed to be witnessing a series of dramas with a well-set stage and a diversity of players," recalled Meredith Nicholson, a prominent Hoosier author at the turn of the century.

"Never any other man stood night after night on stage or platform to receive such solid roars of applause for the reading of poems and for himself," wrote the novelist Booth Tarkington, who was a friend of Riley's. "He did not 'read' his poems; he did not recite them, either; he took his whole body into his hands, as it were, and by his wizard mastery of suggestion left no James Whitcomb Riley at all upon the stage; instead the audiences saw and heard whatever the incomparable comedian wished them to see and hear."

By the late 1880s Riley was in such demand as a speaker that he traveled several months a year giving public readings. But he could not, in his words, "resist the inclination to write," and he continued to supply the *Journal* with poems and to stockpile others for future use. Still wanting desperately to have his work recognized by literary authorities in the East, he also submitted poems to magazines. But the Eastern literary "establishment" continued to ignore him.

In early 1887, however, an editor at the *Century Magazine*, one of the nation's leading literary journals, was greatly impressed with Riley's dialect poem "The Old Man and Jim," about a proud father whose son was killed in the Civil War. The editor invited Riley to New York in November to read his poetry at a program sponsored by the International Copyright League. Immensely flattered, Riley accepted the invitation. Prominent editors and publishers from around the country were scheduled to attend the event, and Riley was to be joined on stage by such distinguished writers as Mark Twain and William Dean Howells. "Is not that a great big and all-swelled-up honor . . . ?" Riley, with his usual good humor, wrote to a friend.

When the Hoosier poet arrived at New York's Chickering

Hall that fall, he knew that many in the vast audience were unfamiliar with his work. James Russell Lowell, one of America's most respected poets, confessed to being "almost a stranger" to Riley's poems. Yet when Riley recited "When the Frost Is on the Punkin," the delighted audience issued "screams of laughter," according to one New York newspaper. And when his performance was over, the crowd was so enthusiastic that he was invited to read again the next day.

The second day's performance was an even greater triumph for Riley. Taking the stage amid thunderous applause, he touched the hearts of many with his tender reading of "Nothin' to Say," a dialect poem about a widowed farmer whose daughter is about to get married. Even before Riley began, however, he scored a victory. Lowell, in introducing him, informed the audience that he had been so impressed with Riley the day before that he stayed up most of the night reading his work. "I can say to you of my own knowledge," the revered literary authority announced, "that you are to have the pleasure of listening to the voice of a true poet."

Lowell's tribute meant a great deal to Riley. It signalled that he had at last been accepted by the nation's literary elite. Other respected writers would soon join Lowell in praising the newspaperman from Indiana, and that praise would continue uninterrupted—and undiminished—for the rest of Riley's life. Newspapers, meanwhile, wrote glowing accounts of Riley's success in New York, and his appeal outside literary circles grew. Soon he was being read in homes from Maine to California. Soon he was being called a poet of national importance. And soon he was being celebrated the way Americans had earlier celebrated Henry Wadsworth Longfellow, the beloved poet who died in 1882.

"There had been dark hours," Riley said, recalling the years he had struggled to win acceptance of his work.

After New York, the "dark hours" were behind him.

* * *

Riley's lecture schedule kept him so busy during the 1880s that he had little time to collect his verses into volumes. By the early 1890s, however, he was determined to make time, and he began what his biographer called "the book-building period." His public readings and the publicity which surrounded his lectures had created a huge demand for his writings; people everywhere wanted a book by the Hoosier poet. To meet the demand, Riley began gathering and revising unpublished poems which he had stuffed in drawers and trunks (he never threw away any of his verses). He also began sorting and grouping poems that had appeared in newspapers and magazines. As he worked, he turned the material over to the Bobbs-Merrill Company of Indianapolis which, with rare exceptions, published at least one Riley book a year from 1890 until his death. In all, ninety books containing Riley's poetry were published by Bobbs-Merrill, with many of them beautifully designed and illustrated—and released just in time for the Christmas gift market.

"They are multiplying by litters, like white mice!" Riley, referring to his books, once wrote to a friend. "There is such a demand in fact that I fear to turn away—lest my luck let up and flop over and die . . . "

Along with "building books," Riley began to settle down and live comfortably during the 1890s. A bachelor, he had never bothered with a permanent residence; when not traveling, he had always lived in boardinghouses or roomed with family members around Indianapolis. "Think of it," he once said. "I never owned a desk in my life and don't know what it is to own a library. Where do I write? Everywhere—sometimes on the kitchen table in my sister's house, then in the parlor and again on the printer's case—just where the fancy seizes me."

By 1893, however, Riley had grown wealthy enough from

his lecture-hall appearances and books that he was able to buy his childhood home in Greenfield. He had always retained fond memories of the green-shuttered "Old Homestead," and he was pleased to have a place where he could gather in the summer with his sisters and brother and their families—a place to live out his belief that "children and loafing and homelife are mighty good things."

That same year, Riley also put down deeper roots in Indianapolis. He could have spent his winters in New York or Boston, where he would have been at the hub of literary activity. But he chose instead to move into a tall brick house at 528 Lockerbie Street, in a quiet, fashionable neighborhood near the downtown district. He had grown to love his adopted city of Indianapolis and viewed it as "high Heaven's sole and only understudy." As for leaving that city or even the state, Riley once wrote to a friend, "No money could tempt me ever to quit my home and people."

Riley was a paying guest at the Lockerbie Street home, which was owned by his friends, Major and Mrs. Charles L. Holstein. Riley shared expenses and bought many items in the house; the residence, where everyone from prominent writers to schoolchildren visited him, eventually came to be seen as his. Soon after his death, a group of his friends bought it from the Holstein family, and today the home operates as a museum where visitors can glimpse how the Hoosier poet spent the last twenty-three years of his life. Upstairs in his second-floor bedroom, a painting of his pet poodle Lockerbie still hangs above the fireplace. His gray pinstripe suits still hang in the closet; his silk top hat sits on the bed. Downstairs, in the drawing room and library, are more of his treasured possessions, including his guitar, a violin he bought for a niece, his easy chair, and his books.

Interestingly, Riley first visited Lockerbie Street in 1880, while taking a stroll one summer evening soon after he moved to Indianapolis. He found the neighborhood to be charming, and on returning to the newspaper office later that night, he wrote a poem about his "discovery." In the next morning's *Journal*, Indianapolis residents awoke to read

> *Such a dear little street it is, nestled away*
> *From the noise of the city and heat of the day,*
> *In cool shady coverts of whispering trees,*
> *With their leaves lifted up to shake hands with the*
>   *breeze*
> *Which in all its wide wanderings never may meet*
> *With a resting-place fairer than Lockerbie Street!*

* * *

Though he continued to tour during the 1890s, Riley did so less frequently; he never enjoyed traveling, and the strain of spending months on the road, lecturing in city after city, began to take its toll on his health. Even when he traveled at a more leisurely pace, however, he rarely made any effort to mingle with local residents or visit sites of interest. Upon arriving in a city, he usually stayed locked in his hotel room, refusing all food and suffering miserably from a case of nerves. His nervousness, fortunately, always disappeared the instant he stepped on stage. But the torture he experienced before each performance was real, and he was always relieved when he could return to Indiana. A lecture tour, he once said, was "a distress to my soul."

Home didn't always bring relief, however. Often lonely, Riley suffered bouts of depression and boredom. As an escape, he drank—too often and too much. He knew that his drinking binges hurt his creativity, so he would force himself to go stretches without touching liquor. But he struggled with alcoholism throughout his life, something his family members and closest friends never talked about publicly and something not widely known to his many admirers.

Unlike the drinking, Riley's other habits and personality traits were no secret. Caring only for poetry, he had no interest in politics or social trends. As his friend Meredith Nicholson noted, he was as "unconscious" of world events "as though he lived on another planet." He voted only once in his life, and that was as a favor to a friend, who was a candidate for a local office. Ironically, Riley became so confused when marking his ballot that he ended up voting for his friend's opponent.

His reputation for getting lost was also well known. When he traveled, he constantly relied on someone else to tell him which train to take and when to get off. "I'm the blamedst fool travelin', I reckon, they is outside o' the durn lunatic asylum— 'bout not gittin' trains, er gittin' the wrong one . . . ," Riley once humorously wrote a friend. Upon arriving in a particular city, he wasn't much better with directions. When in Philadelphia once to have his portrait painted by the famous artist John Singer Sargent, Riley had to rely on an escort each day to lead him to the studio.

Still, Riley's odd behavior didn't seem to bother those who knew and admired him. Friends valued his gentleness and boyish playfulness. They appreciated his sympathy and tolerance. And they treasured his wit. "Everybody who read Riley loved him, and those who met him loved him even more," said Yale University professor William Lyon Phelps, who knew Riley well for nearly twenty years. "He never disappointed you; he was the man of his works. He was simple, affectionate, true-hearted; and his humor was the ground quality of his personality."

* * *

By the turn of the century, Riley was still making books, but he filled them largely with poems written years earlier. His urge to create was gone. Gone, too, was his interest in touring. His health, never good, had begun to fail, and he preferred more and more the comforts of what he called "Lockerbie Land."

His popularity remained high, however, and honors were heaped upon him. Literary societies such as the National Institute of Arts and Letters elected him to membership. Colleges and universities awarded him degrees. Hoosier schoolchildren celebrated his birthday with special programs. And in 1915, the National Commissioner of Education declared that October 7 was to be observed as "Riley Day" throughout the nation's schools, in honor of the poet's sixty-sixth birthday.

All those outpourings of affection were slight, however, compared to the public's response to his death on July 22, 1916. The news that he had died at home in his sleep was reported in newspapers around the world. President Woodrow Wilson sent condolences to the family. The Speaker of the U.S. House of Representatives issued a statement expressing the nation's loss. In Indiana, flags were lowered to half mast, and communities planned memorial services. In Indianapolis, where his body was permitted to lie in state under the dome of the capitol building, thirty-five thousand mourners filed past his casket to pay their last respects.

His burial site, which to this day is still visited by many Hoosiers, is marked by a marble tomb in Crown Hill Cemetery, at the top of the highest hill in the city.

When modern literary critics are asked to list the "great" poets of the nineteenth century, they begin with Walt Whitman and Emily Dickinson. When asked to name "important" poets critics usually mention Longfellow, Lowell, Poe, William Cullen Bryant, and John Greenleaf Whittier. If Riley's name comes up at all, he's quickly dismissed as "minor."

Yet the men and women of Riley's generation thought there was nothing "minor" about him. He was their spokesman, the poet who understood them and whom they could understand. He immortalized their simple virtues. He celebrated their natural speech. He recaptured the joys and sorrows of their childhood. He recorded their lives—on farms, in villages, in countless small towns.

Though Americans everywhere could identify with Riley's work, the people of Indiana claimed him with special pride. He was the "Hoosier Poet," and as author Edgar Lee Masters noted many years ago, Riley "put Indiana as a place and a people in the memory of America, more thoroughly and more permanently than has been done by any other poet before or since his day . . ."

SUGGESTIONS FOR FURTHER READING

Crowder, Richard. *Those Innocent Years: The Legacy and Inheritance of a Hero of the Victorian Era, James Whitcomb Riley*. Indianapolis: The Bobbs-Merrill Company, Inc., 1957.

Dickey, Marcus. *The Youth of James Whitcomb Riley*. Indianapolis: The Bobbs-Merrill Company, 1919.

Dickey, Marcus. *The Maturity of James Whitcomb Riley*. Indianapolis: The Bobbs-Merrill Company, 1922.

Manlove, Donald C., editor. *The Best of James Whitcomb Riley*. Bloomington: Indiana University Press, 1982.

Nicholson, Meredith. *The Hoosiers*. New York: The Macmillan Company, 1900.

Nicholson, Meredith. *The Man in the Street*. New York: Charles Scribner's Sons, 1921.

Nolan, Jeannette Covert, Horace Gregory, and James T. Farrell. *Poet of the People: An Evaluation of James Whitcomb Riley*. Bloomington: Indiana University Press, 1951.

Phelps, William Lyon, editor. *Letters of James Whitcomb Riley*. Indianapolis: The Bobbs-Merrill Company, 1917.

Revell, Peter. *James Whitcomb Riley*. New York: Twayne Publishers, Inc., 1970.

NOTHIN' TO SAY

Nothin' to say, my daughter! Nothin' at all to say!
Gyrls that's in love, I've noticed, giner'ly has their way!
Yer mother did, afore you, when her folks objected to
  me—
Yit here I am and here you air! and yer mother—where
  is she?

You look lots like yer mother: purty much same in size;
And about the same complected; and favor about the
  eyes:
Like her, too, about livin' here, because *she* couldn't
  stay;
It'll most seem like you was dead like her!—but I hain't
  got nothin' to say!

She left you her little Bible—writ yer name acrost the
  page—
And left her ear-bobs fer you, ef ever you come of age;
I've alluz kep' 'em and gyuarded 'em, but ef yer goin'
  away—
Nothin' to say, my daughter! Nothin' at all to say!

You don't rickollect her, I reckon? No: you wasn't a year
  old then!
And now yer—how old *air* you? W'y, child, not "*twenty*"!
  When?
And yer nex' birthday's in Aprile? and you want to git
  married that day?
I wisht yer mother was livin'!—but I hain't got nothin'
  to say!

Twenty year! and as good a gyrl as parent ever found!
There's a straw ketched on to yer dress there—I'll bresh
  it off—turn round.
(Her mother was jes' twenty when us two run away.)
Nothin' to say, my daughter! Nothin' at all to say!

WHEN THE FROST IS ON THE PUNKIN

When the frost is on the punkin and the fodder's in the
  shock,
And you hear the kyouck and gobble of the struttin'
  turkey-cock,
And the clackin' of the guineys, and the cluckin' of the
  hens,
And the rooster's hallylooyer as he tiptoes on the fence;
O, it's then's the times a feller is a-feelin' at his best,
With the risin' sun to greet him from a night of peaceful
  rest,
As he leaves the house, bareheaded, and goes out to
  feed the stock,
When the frost is on the punkin and the fodder's in the
  shock.

They's something kindo' harty-like about the atmusfere
When the heat of summer's over and the coolin' fall is
  here—
Of course we miss the flowers, and the blossums on the
  trees,
And the mumble of the hummin'-birds and buzzin' of
  the bees;
But the air's so appetizin'; and the landscape through
  the haze
Of a crisp and sunny morning of the airly autumn days
Is a pictur' that no painter has the colorin' to mock—
When the frost is on the punkin and the fodder's in the
  shock.

The husky, rusty russel of the tossels of the corn,
And the raspin' of the tangled leaves, as golden as the
  morn;
The stubble in the furries—kindo' lonesome-like, but
  still
A-preachin' sermons to us of the barns they growed to
  fill;

The strawstack in the medder, and the reaper in the
    shed;
The hosses in theyr stall below—the clover overhead!—
O, it sets my hart a-clickin' like the tickin' of a clock,
When the frost is on the punkin and the fodder's in the
    shock!

Then your apples all is gethered, and the ones a feller
    keeps
Is poured around the celler-floor in red and yeller
    heaps;
And your cider-makin' 's over, and your wimmern-folks
    is through
With their mince and apple-butter, and theyr souse and
    sausage, too!. . .
I don't know how to tell it—but ef sich a thing could be
As the Angels wantin' boardin', and they'd call around
    on *me*—
I'd want to 'commodate 'em—all the whole-indurin'
    flock—
When the frost is on the punkin and the fodder's in the
    shock!

LITTLE ORPHANT ANNIE

Little Orphant Annie's come to our house to stay,
An' wash the cups an' saucers up, an' brush the
    crumbs away,
An' shoo the chickens off the porch, an' dust the
    hearth, an' sweep,
An' make the fire, an' bake the bread, an' earn her
    board-an'-keep;
An' all us other children, when the supper-things is
    done,
We set around the kitchen fire an' has the mostest
    fun
A-list'nin' to the witch-tales 'at Annie tells about,
    An' the Gobble-uns 'at gits you
            Ef you
                Don't
                    Watch
                        Out!

Wunst they wuz a little boy wouldn't say his
    prayers,—
An' when he went to bed at night, away up stairs,
His Mammy heerd him holler, an' his Daddy heerd
    him bawl,
An' when they turn't the kivvers down, he wuzn't
    there at all!
An' they seeked him in the rafter-room, an' cubby
    hole, an' press,
An' seeked him up the chimbly-flue, an' ever'wheres,
    I guess;
But all they ever found wuz thist his pants an' round-
    about:—
    An' the Gobble-uns'll git you
            Ef you
                Don't
                    Watch
                        Out!

An' one time a little girl 'ud allus laugh an' grin,
An' make fun of ever'one, an' all her blood an' kin;
An' wunst, when they was "company," an' ole folks
  wuz there,
She mocked 'em an' shocked 'em, an' said she didn't
  care!
An' thist as she kicked her heels, an' turn't to run an'
  hide,
They wuz two great big Black Things a-standin' by
  her side,
An' they snatched her through the ceilin' 'fore she
  knowed what she's about!
   An' the Gobble-uns'll git you
        Ef you
           Don't
              Watch
                 Out!

An' little Orphant Annie says, when the blaze is blue,
An' the lamp-wick sputters, an' the wind goes *woo-oo*!
An' you hear the crickets quit, an' the moon is gray,
An' the lightnin'-bugs in dew is all squenched away,
You better mind yer parunts an' yer teachers fond an'
  dear,
An' churish them 'at loves you, an' dry the orphant's
  tear,
An' he'p the pore an' needy ones 'at clusters all about,
   Er the Gobble-uns'll git you
        Ef you
           Don't
              Watch
                 Out!

THE RAGGEDY MAN

O the Raggedy Man! He works fer Pa;
An' he's the goodest man ever you saw!
He comes to our house every day,
An' waters the horses, an' feeds 'em hay;
An' he opens the shed—an' we all ist laugh
When he drives out our little old wobble-ly calf;
An' nen—ef our hired girl says he can—
He milks the cow fer 'Lizabuth Ann.—
    Ain't he a' awful good Raggedy Man?
        Raggedy! Raggedy! Raggedy Man!

W'y, The Raggedy Man—he's ist so good,
He splits the kindlin' an' chops the wood;
An' nen he spades in our garden, too,
An' does most things 'at *boys* can't do!—
He clumbed clean up in our big tree
An' shooked a' apple down fer me—
An' nother'n', too, fer 'Lizabuth Ann—
An' nother'n', too, fer The Raggedy Man.—
    Ain't he a' awful kind Raggedy Man?
        Raggedy! Raggedy! Raggedy Man!

An' The Raggedy Man one time say he
Pick' roast' rambos from a' orchurd-tree,
An' et em—all ist roast' an' hot!—
An' it's so, too!—'cause a corn-crib got
Afire one time an' all burn' down
On "The Smoot Farm," 'bout four mile from town—
On "The Smoot Farm"! Yes—an' the hired han'
'At worked there nen 'uz The Raggedy Man!—
    Ain't he the beatin'est Raggedy Man?
        Raggedy! Raggedy! Raggedy Man!

The Raggedy Man's so good an' kind
He'll be our "horsey," an' "haw" an' mind
Ever'thing 'at you make him do—

An' won't run off—'less you want him to!
I drived him wunst way down our lane
An' he got skeered, when it 'menced to rain,
An' ist rared up an' squealed and run
Purt' nigh away!—an' it's all in fun!
Nen he skeered *ag'in* at a' old tin can . . .
    Whoa! y' old runaway Raggedy Man!
        Raggedy! Raggedy! Raggedy Man!

An' The Raggedy Man, he knows most rhymes
An' tells 'em, ef I be good, sometimes:
Knows 'bout Giunts, an' Griffuns, an' Elves,
An' the Squidgicum-Squees 'at swallers ther'selves!
An', wite by the pump in our pasture-lot,
He showed me the hole 'at the Wunks is got,
'At lives 'way deep in the ground, an' can
Turn into me, er 'Lizabuth Ann,
Er Ma er Pa er The Raggedy Man!
    Ain't he a funny old Raggedy Man?
        Raggedy! Raggedy! Raggedy Man!

An' wunst, when The Raggedy Man come late,
An' pigs ist root' thue the garden-gate,
He 'tend like the pigs 'us *bears* an' said,
"Old Bear-shooter'll shoot 'em dead!"
An' race' an' chase' 'em, an' they'd ist run
When he pint his hoe at 'em like it's a gun
An' go "Bang!—Bang!" nen 'tend he stan'
An' load up his gun ag'in! Raggedy Man!
    He's an old Bear-Shooter Raggedy Man!
        Raggedy! Raggedy! Raggedy Man!

An' sometimes The Raggedy Man lets on
We're little *prince*-children, an' old King's gone
To git more money, an' lef' us there—
And *Robbers* is ist thick ever'where;
An' nen—ef we all won't cry, fer *shore*—
The Raggedy Man he'll come and "splore
The Castul-Halls," an' steal the "gold"—

An steal *us*, too, an' grab an' hold
An' pack us off to his old "Cave"!—An'
   Haymow's the "cave" o' The Raggedy Man!
      Raggedy! Raggedy! Raggedy Man!

The Raggedy Man—one time when he
Wus makin' a little bow-n'-orry fer me,
Says "When *you're* big like your Pa is,
Air *you* go' to keep a fine store like his
An be a rich merchunt—an' wear fine clothes?—
Er what *air* you go' to be, goodness knows!"
An' nen he laughed at 'Lizabuth Ann,
An' I says " 'M go' to be a Raggedy Man!—
   I'm ist go' to be a nice Raggedy Man!"
      Raggedy! Raggedy! Raggedy Man!

LOCKERBIE STREET

Such a dear little street it is, nestled away
From the noise of the city and heat of the day,
In cool shady coverts of whispering trees,
With their leaves lifted up to shake hands with the
    breeze
Which in all its wide wanderings never may meet
With a resting-place fairer than Lockerbie Street!

There is such a relief, from the clangor and din
Of the heart of the town, to go loitering in
Through the dim, narrow walks, with the sheltering
    shade
Of the trees waving over the long promenade,
And littering lightly the ways of our feet
With the gold of the sunshine of Lockerbie Street.

And the nights that come down the dark pathways of
    dusk,
With the stars in their tresses, and odors of musk
In their moon-woven raiments, bespangled with
    dews,
And looped up with lilies for lovers to use
In the songs that they sing to the tinkle and beat
Of their sweet serenadings through Lockerbie Street.

O my Lockerbie Street! You are fair to be seen—
Be it noon of the day, or the rare and serene
Afternoon of the night—you are one to my heart,
And I love you above all the phrases of art,
For no language could frame and no lips could repeat
My rhyme-haunted raptures of Lockerbie Street.

JAMES WHITCOMB RILEY loved to read, and as a young boy his favorite book was a collection of poems by Henry Wadsworth Longfellow, the most famous American poet of the 1800s.

Born in New England in 1807, Longfellow began his writing career in the 1830s while teaching at Harvard College in Cambridge, Massachusetts. His best-loved poems included "The Children's Hour," "The Village Blacksmith," and "Paul Revere's Ride." He was also known for long narrative poems that included "Evangeline," "The Song of Hiawatha," and "The Courtship of Miles Standish." Popular in Europe as well as in America, Longfellow was treated like a celebrity wherever he went. By the end of the century, his poems had been translated into a dozen languages.

Riley's admiration for Longfellow lasted well beyond his boyhood. As an aspiring poet, the Hoosier verse-maker continued to read the scholarly Longfellow and to carry a book of his poetry whenever he traveled. Riley enjoyed Longfellow's poems because they were written in a clear, graceful style. He also liked Longfellow's optimism, something he found missing in the works of other nineteenth-century American poets such as Edgar Allan Poe and Walt Whitman.

Henry Wadsworth Longfellow

"Longfellow is my poetry Bible," he once said. "To read him is a liberal education. The beauty of his character transcends everything else. Outside of the excellence of his poems, his is the sweetest human mind that ever existed."

In 1876, while despairing over whether he had any literary talent, the twenty-seven-year-old Riley sent three of his poems to Longfellow. Longfellow promptly responded that he had read the poems "with great pleasure" and thought that they showed "the true poetic faculty and insight." Buoyed by the encouragement, Riley kept writing.

Five years later, Longfellow and Riley met for the first and only time. Riley's fame as a poet had spread beyond the Midwest, and he was invited to give a reading in Boston, an appearance that paved the way for national recognition of his work. A few days before Riley performed at Boston's Tremont Temple, he worked up his courage and made an unannounced visit to Longfellow's home in Cambridge. Longfellow, who was seventy-four and in ill health, greeted the Hoosier poet warmly and recalled the poems that Riley had sent him years earlier. He then paid Riley the highest of compliments by asking him to read some of his verses. Honored, Riley recited "Old-Fashioned Roses."

Three months after that visit, Longfellow died. For the rest of his life, Riley would look upon Longfellow as one of the world's greatest poets and would recommend his work to other aspiring writers. Americans, meanwhile, would increasingly look to Riley as Longfellow's successor, and they would shower him with the affection they had once reserved for the bard from New England.

"He [Riley] took by divine right," a critic for the *New York Sun* wrote many years ago, "the place as an American poet which has not been occupied since Longfellow's tenancy ended."

OLD-FASHIONED ROSES

They ain't no style about 'em,
And they're sort o' pale and faded
Yit the doorway here, without 'em,
Would be lonesomer, and shaded
With a good 'eal blacker shadder
Than the morning-glories makes,
And the sunshine would look sadder
Fer their good old-fashion' sakes.

AMONG THE MANY WAYS Indiana sought to honor Riley after his death was to establish in 1924 a children's hospital in Indianapolis. Today the James Whitcomb Riley Hospital for Children is one of the ten largest children's hospitals in the United States and the only one in Indiana dedicated exclusively to the care of young people. One of its primary missions is to treat children with the most complicated medical problems. Patients range from newborns with breathing problems to adolescents stricken with cancer, from burn victims to youngsters needing heart or kidney transplants.

Each year nearly eight thousand children are admitted to the hospital, and thousands more receive treatment at Riley's outpatient clinics. Riley is especially equipped to treat the youngest of the young; half of the patients are less than two years old, and many are less than two months old.

The hospital, which today is managed in conjunction with Indiana University, was established through the efforts of the James Whitcomb Riley Memorial Association. The association was founded in 1921 to honor the Hoosier poet, as well as to promote a love of history and to improve the lives of Indiana's children. Organizers included some of Riley's closest friends: the journalist and playwright George Ade, the novelist Booth Tarkington, the author and diplomat Meredith Nicholson, and Riley's publisher William C. Bobbs.

As the hospital grew in size and prestige, the association began looking for other ways to build on Riley's reputation as a lover of children. In 1955 it opened a camp for physically disabled youth. Today Camp Riley, located on twenty-three hundred acres of woods in Morgan County south of Indianapolis, continues to serve as a model recreation center for the handicapped. Children of all ages, and with a wide range of disabilities, go there each year to swim, fish, canoe, study nature, and pursue other outdoor activities.

What would James Whitcomb Riley think of all these efforts to help young people? In his poetry he often wrote about children who needed looking after—orphans, a crippled boy,

Built in the 1920s, Riley Hospital for Children continues to expand with the times.

a dying baby, a frightened runaway, rough-and-tumble youngsters with grimy faces and shabby clothes. He never made fun of or ridiculed his young fictional creations. Rather, he seemed to have a special affection for them and, whether it was the child who was stung by a bumblebee or the little girl with a lisp, he showed them a special sympathy.

"I believe *all* childern's good, ef they're only *understood*," Riley once wrote in a poem. If he were still living, he likely would approve of all the good that Riley Hospital and Camp Riley supporters are trying to do for today's "childern."

Elizabeth Riley.

Captain Reuben Riley.

Log cabin on the
National Road where
Riley was born.

The Old Homestead in Greenfield.

Riley at age 22.

Trademark designed by Riley for
McCrillus' Standard Remedies.

An 1879 program cover in which Riley is listed as a speaker.

Riley with his young nephew Edmund Eitel and the author Hamlin Garland at the Greenfield Homestead in 1894.

The original "Old Swimmin'-Hole" with Riley (wearing a black hat) and two friends on the bank.

Riley's home on Lockerbie Street in Indianapolis.

Riley posed for Mary Lyon Taylor, an Indianapolis pictorialist, around 1907.

Schoolchildren in Libertyville, Indiana, wish Riley a happy birthday—his sixty-fourth—in 1913.

Riley, accustomed to being greeted everywhere by children, shakes the hand of unidentified girl while in a touring car with Governor Ralston and Indianapolis Mayor Bell in 1915.

Gene Stratton-Porter

3

GENE STRATTON-PORTER

IF you want to know me, my books are the best way, for
. . . they furnish a better biography than I can write.

—Gene Stratton-Porter, 1908

P ICTURE A DETERMINED WOMAN in hip boots toting a gun
and lugging camera equipment deep into a swamp in-
fested with rattlesnakes. The swamp is dark, gloomy
and oozing with muck. Owls hoot and screech. Frogs bellow.
Muskrats dart. Mosquitoes, millions of them, swarm above
the foul-smelling, murky waters.

Around the turn of the century a vast, primeval swamp
called the Limberlost covered a portion of eastern Indiana
south of Fort Wayne. Because of the dangers lurking there,
few people ever ventured near the Limberlost. Few, that is,
except Gene Stratton-Porter. She went there regularly to
photograph birds and other wildlife and to take notes for her
many books—books in which she shared her love of nature
with readers around the world.

During the first two decades of the 1900s, Gene Stratton-
Porter was one of America's best-loved writers. Her novels
about the great outdoors, which included best-sellers such as
Freckles and *A Girl of the Limberlost*, sold millions of copies.
And her nature books, in which she described the birds, in-

sects, and plants of Indiana's woods and swamps, had a loyal following of readers. By 1915 her books were selling at such a staggering rate that someone estimated they would, if piled one atop another, be sixteen hundred times higher than the world's tallest building.

But it wasn't just as a nature writer that Stratton-Porter left her mark. She was a skilled nature photographer whose pioneering work in capturing birds on print influenced photographers who followed her. She was also a leader in a new movement to protect and preserve the nation's natural resources. Throughout America at the turn of the century, people were leaving family farms and moving to cities to work in factories. In the process, wildlife and wild places were being destroyed to make room for new roads, newer industries, and bigger communities. Stratton-Porter wasn't opposed to all the changes occurring around her. But she believed passionately that Americans needed to respect the natural world as they pursued economic growth. Through her many books and magazine articles she urged people to live in harmony with their environment and not to "madly and recklessly" destroy nature's gifts.

Today a new generation of readers is embracing Stratton-Porter's ecological message. People concerned about the environment are finding that her warnings against draining wetlands, destroying vegetation, and upsetting the balance of nature have special relevance in our modern age—especially as Americans struggle to clean up polluted rivers, purify dirty air, save animals from extinction, and avoid a much-feared energy crisis.

But environmentalists aren't the only ones who continue to find Gene Stratton-Porter's books interesting. Her novels, though not read nearly as much as they once were, still appeal to people who like sentiment and romance. And readers weary of violence and gloom find her fiction refreshingly wholesome and upbeat, just as the author intended.

"I have done every one of my books from my heart's best

impulses, made them as clean and decent as I know how, and as beautiful and as interesting," Stratton-Porter once wrote. "I never have spared myself in the least degree, mind or body, when it came to giving the best I was able . . ."

* * *

Geneva, later known as Gene, was born on a farm in Wabash County, Indiana, on August 17, 1863. She was the youngest of twelve children born to Mark and Mary Stratton. The Stratton farm was called Hopewell, and, according to Gene, "no other farm was ever quite so lovely." It sat on rolling land, covered by forest and tilled fields and crossed by three streams. Near the farmhouse was a garden where Gene's mother, who had "flower magic in her fingers," grew tulips, lilies, daffodils, and dahlias. Beyond that was an orchard, rich in the spring with the fragrance of apple, peach, and pear trees.

By today's standards, life in Indiana in the 1860s wasn't easy. But Gene's parents had worked hard to establish their farmstead out of Hoosier wilderness. By the time of Gene's birth, the farm was prospering and the family lived comfortably. As Gene would later note, "The days of pioneer struggles were past."

Early in Gene's childhood, her mother contracted typhoid fever and never fully recovered from her illness. Though Mary Stratton continued to teach Gene about plants, it was Mark Stratton, a farmer and part-time preacher, who took charge of rearing the couple's energetic daughter. Gene would follow him on his daily chores, sometimes napping in fence corners while he and her brothers worked, other times running freely through meadows and woods. From her father, Gene learned that plants and animals were a gift of God and deserving of care and respect. From Mark Stratton, too, Gene learned how to deal gently with wild creatures, and before long she was making pets of baby squirrels and rabbits, feeding sweetened water to butterflies, and nursing wounded animals back to health.

As she moved about in her outdoor school, Gene developed a special love for birds, a fondness that would last a lifetime and earn her the nickname "Bird Woman." She was fascinated by swallows, larks, pigeons, red-winged blackbirds, wrens, woodpeckers, blue jays. "From my earliest recollection," she wrote years later, "I was the friend and devoted champion of every bird that nested in the garden, on the fences, on the ground, in the bushes, in the dooryard, or in the orchard trees. From breakfast until dinner and from dinner until supper, almost my entire day was spent in making the rounds of these nests, watching the birds while they built, brooded, or fed their young . . ."

Of all the birds that she came to know, she envied the red-tailed hawks most of all. Catching sight of them up among the clouds, she couldn't help but think of their freedom— something she valued dearly in her own life. "I envied these birds their power to soar in the face of the wind, to ride with the stiff gale of a beating storm, or to hang motionless as if frozen in air, according to their will, as I envied nothing else on earth."

When Gene was eleven years old, her family moved to the neighboring town of Wabash, so that her mother could receive better medical care. Although Mary Stratton died soon afterwards, the family continued to live in Wabash, where Gene was enrolled in school. She never liked the classroom and resented that teachers never "made the slightest effort to discover what I cared for personally." Their only goal, she later recalled, was to push her "into the groove into which all other pupils ran." Still, to please her father, Gene continued her schooling at Wabash High School. But in the spring of 1883 at age nineteen, she dropped out before graduating. Years later she insisted she had few regrets:

Unlike most school children, I studied harder after

leaving school than ever before, and in a manner that did me real good. I never went to school again, and the best that can be said of what education I have is that it was strictly private. It was the very best kind in the world for me . . . I studied the things in which I was most interested . . .

Though Gene loved being free of the classroom, she found herself increasingly frustrated by another matter: other young women didn't share her interest in wildlife. Her peers preferred to embroider, paint, or daintily fan themselves in the family parlor—behavior considered proper for ladies of that era—rather than to tramp through forests in search of berries, row a boat across a lake to gather water lilies, or follow willow-fringed rivers to study birds. As Gene recalled years later, "I was considered an outcast, half demented because I fished in the rain one night when I might have attended a ball. One woman blasted me with scorn because I had the hardihood to offer to her a timothy straw strung with luscious big, wild red raspberries."

Still, even though some people regarded her as odd, Gene had no desire to change her ways. She would, throughout her life, take pride in being different. And years later she would write: "I came in time to believe that there might be a life work for one woman in leading these other women back to the forest"—back to an understanding of and appreciation for the outdoor world.

* * *

In 1884, shortly before she turned twenty-one, Gene visited Sylvan Lake at Rome City, home of one of the most popular resorts in northern Indiana. Charles Dorwin Porter, a druggist who was vacationing in the area, spotted her walking around the resort, and later he wrote her a letter asking

SCHOOLHOUSES ARE made wrong. If they must be, they should be built in a woods pasture beside a stream, where you could wade, swim, and be comfortable in summer, and slide and skate in winter. The windows should be cut to the floor, and stand wide open, so the birds and butterflies could pass through. You ought to learn your geography by climbing a hill, walking through a valley, wading creeks, making islands in them, and promontories, capes, and peninsulas along the bank. You should do your arithmetic sitting under trees adding hickorynuts, subtracting walnuts, multiplying butternuts, and dividing hazelnuts. You could use apples for fractions, and tin cups for liquid measure. You could spell everything in sight and this would teach you the words that are really used in the world.

—*Laddie: A True Blue Story*, 1913

UPON HER MARRIAGE to Charles Dorwin Porter in April 1886, Gene assumed the name "Mrs. Porter." However, in a show of independence that was unusual for women of that era, she insisted on using her maiden name in her books and articles, identifying herself as Gene Stratton-Porter.

Gene was not quite twenty-three when she married the thirty-six-year-old druggist from Adams County. An old family friend described her at the time as "romantically beautiful, tall and stately, with a distinguished air, and with a carriage and walk that was superb."

if they could correspond. Gene agreed, and a romance bloomed. In April 1886, after an eighteen-month courtship, the two were married.

The Porters lived first in Decatur near Fort Wayne. Then in 1888 they moved eighteen miles south to a village that, interestingly enough, was named Geneva. Charles Porter operated a successful drugstore there, and within a few blocks of the store the couple eventually built a large two-story home which Stratton-Porter called a "cabin," but which was actually the finest and most expensive residence in town. There, Stratton-Porter reared the couple's only child Jeannette. There, too, she began to think about a career.

Less than a mile from the Porters' new home was the Limberlost Swamp, a vast area of marshlands, streams, lakes, and unbroken forest where wildlife flourished. In the winter, when the swamp was draped with snow and frost, it had what Stratton-Porter called a "lacy exquisite beauty." But from May until October it was, in her words, "practically tropical jungle."

By the late 1800s lumbermen, seeking to cut the swamp's timber for ship masts and fine furniture, had begun building roads around the Limberlost's border. But travel into the dark interior remained nearly impossible. As Stratton-Porter would later write: "A Limberlost trip at that time was not to be joked about. It had not been shorn, branded or tamed. There were most excellent reasons why I should not go there . . . In its physical aspect it was a treacherous swamp and quagmire filled with every plant, animal and human danger known . . . in the Central States."

Charles Porter, not surprisingly, urged his wife to stay away from that uncharted wilderness. But Stratton-Porter, attracted to the colorful birds she saw flashing through the treetops of the Limberlost and still valuing her independence, was drawn to that ghostly world. Before long she was making regular trips there, dressed in knee-high leather hiking boots, a khaki-colored skirt that blended with the trees, and a hat draped with mosquito netting. Local townspeople, catching sight of her little black horse and buggy on the road, would shake their heads in disbelief.

For protection against snakes lurking in the shallow waters, Stratton-Porter usually carried a gun on her field trips. She almost always carried a camera. She had become interested in photography after her daughter Jeannette gave her a small camera as a Christmas gift in 1895. The Limberlost was a perfect place to photograph winged creatures in their natural setting, and Stratton-Porter, who earlier had sketched birds, now went to great lengths to record them through a camera lens.

To get the close-up photographs she wanted, she worked first to gain the birds' trust. Just as she had done as a child on her family's farm, she would visit nests every day, always inching closer until the parents became accustomed to her presence. Sometimes she would chase away squirrels or snakes; other times, she'd drop food in the nests. Eventually she would set up her camera, often concealing it behind branches or using stepladders and ropes to rig her bulky equipment from trees. Incredibly patient, she then would sit and wait, hoping and watching for just the right picture.

"I have reproduced birds in moments of fear, anger, in full tide of song, while dressing their plumage, taking a sun bath, courting, feeding their young," she once wrote. "The recipe for such studies is: Go slow, know birds and understand them, and remain in the woods until . . . they will be perfectly natural in your presence."

Of the many stories Stratton-Porter told about exploring the swamp, one vividly illustrates how devoted she was to photographing creatures in the wild. She received a message one day that lumbermen had spotted a baby bird, white and soft as a powder puff, in a hollow elm tree. Beside the bird was a large, pale blue egg with brown speckles. Her curiosity aroused, Stratton-Porter set off with her husband into one of the most dangerous parts of the Limberlost. She later wrote about finding the rare nest, home to a family of black vultures—birds she had never before seen in Indiana:

> I shielded my camera in my arms . . . At the well we
> started on foot, Mr. Porter in kneeboots, I in waist-high
> waders. The time was late June; we forced our way
> between steaming, fetid pools, through swarms of
> gnats, flies, mosquitoes, poisonous insects, keeping a
> sharp watch for rattlesnakes. We sank ankle deep at
> every step, and logs we thought solid broke under us.
> Our progress was a steady succession of prying and
> pulling each other to the surface. Our clothing was
> wringing wet, and the exposed parts of our bodies
> lumpy with bites and stings. My husband found the
> tree, cleared the opening to the great prostrate log, tra-
> versed its unspeakable odours for nearly forty feet to
> its farthest recess, and brought the baby and egg to the
> light in his leaf-lined hat.
>   We could endure the location only by dipping nap-
> kins in deodorant and binding them over our mouths
> and nostrils. Every third day for almost three months
> we made this trip . . .

* * *

By the early 1900s, Stratton-Porter had mastered her camera well enough that her nature photographs were being
published in outdoor magazines. But by then she was also
trying to master a new craft—writing. She had had some
success writing about birds and wildlife for magazines. She
had even had some of her short stories published. When a
magazine editor suggested she expand one of her manuscripts
and submit it to a book publisher, she followed that advice—
and then celebrated. In the spring of 1903 the Bobbs-Merrill
Company of Indianapolis published *The Song of the Cardinal*, just as the homemaker-turned-author was about to turn
forty.

Stratton-Porter's inspiration for *The Song of the Cardinal* came while she was walking outdoors one afternoon. She spotted on the road the limp body of a redbird shot by a hunter on target practice. Outraged at such a senseless killing, Stratton-Porter took the bird home to bury it. By the time she had finished scooping a deep grave, she had in her head the outline of a story—one featuring a lovesick cardinal who lived at the edge of the Limberlost and who narrowly escaped a hunter's bullet.

"It is the sort of book I love to write," she wrote a few years after its release. "Clean, true to nature and . . . illustrated with my own pictures so that they really help out the text."

Readers liked the book, especially the descriptions of Indiana's woodlands and wetlands. But sales were slow and limited to a small audience. Determined to appeal to more readers, Stratton-Porter immediately began a second novel focusing on people rather than birds. She kept the Limberlost as the setting for her story. She even created a character, a "Bird Woman," who loved to photograph birds in the swamp. But the story's action centered around a good-hearted orphan named Freckles who guarded the Limberlost's valuable timber from thieves and who fell in love with a pretty girl called the Swamp Angel.

Freckles was published in 1904, and as with Stratton-Porter's first novel, sales were slow at first. But that changed as readers discovered that *Freckles* wasn't strictly a nature book, but rather a light romance with an outdoor setting. Soon sales began to soar. And soon Stratton-Porter's mailbox was stuffed with letters from admiring readers across America, many of them thanking her for such a wholesome and uplifting tale. One of her favorite letters was from the scholar, clergyman, and lawyer Oren Root who, after reading her book in one evening, wrote: "I have a severe cold this morning, because I got my feet very wet last night, walking the trail with 'Freckles,' but I am willing to risk pneumonia any time for another book like that."

NIGHT CLOSED IN. The Limberlost stirred gently, then shook herself, growled, and awoke about him.

There seemed to be a great owl hooting from every hollow tree and a little one screeching from every knothole. The bellowing of monster bullfrogs was not sufficiently deafening to shut out the wailing of whippoor-wills that seemed to come from every bush. Night-hawks swept past him with their shivering cry, and bats struck his face. A prowling wildcat missed its catch and screamed with rage. A lost fox bayed incessantly for its mate.

The hair on the back of Freckles' neck rose like bristles, and his knees wavered beneath him. He could not see if the dreaded snakes were on the trail, nor, in the pandemonium, hear the rattle for which McLean had cautioned him to listen. He stood rooted to the ground in an agony of fear. His breath whistled between his teeth. The perspiration ran down his face and body in little streams.

—*Freckles*, 1904

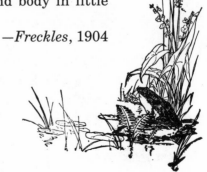

* * *

Four years after the publication of *Freckles*, Stratton-Porter assessed her literary success this way: "You cannot honestly say that I am wildly popular . . ."

An accurate remark, perhaps, in 1908. But from 1909 to 1915, Stratton-Porter turned out one best-selling book after another. And by the time America entered World War I, she was wildly popular throughout the country, not to mention in countries around the world.

Her best-loved books were her novels, which included *A Girl of the Limberlost* (1909), *The Harvester* (1911), *Laddie* (1913), and *Michael O'Halloran* (1915). But her nature books—straightforward accounts of her work outdoors—were also enjoyed by appreciative fans. Together, both her fiction and nonfiction sold for many years at a rate of nearly seventeen hundred copies a day. And in the United States alone, publishers estimated she had a following of fifty million readers. By the 1920s, she and her books were such a part of American life that William Lyon Phelps, the respected educator and literary critic, declared: "She is a public institution, like Yellowstone Park."

Overseas, her fans were nearly as numerous—and just as enthusiastic. From London, England, a businessman sent word that "your books are among my valued possessions." From Peking, China, an English teacher wrote that her books were a "blessing." From a continent away, a professor's wife wanted Stratton-Porter to know "what pleasure and profit your works are to many in Africa." And from Australia, a schoolgirl shared that she and her "chums" gathered to discuss their favorite characters in Stratton-Porter's novels. "I think," the letter-writer added, "you must be a wonderful woman to write such beautiful books . . . They have helped me very much."

Stratton-Porter's passion for nature, combined with her gift for storytelling, is what made her fictional work so enormously appealing. In novel after novel, she offered readers a "whiff of the outdoors" by describing flowers, trees, vines, birds, insects, and other wild creatures. She also created characters who had a special connection to the natural world. In *A Girl of the Limberlost* the heroine Elnora Comstock collects moths from the swamp to pay for her schooling. In *The Harvester* a woodsman earns his living selling herbs and seeds to be used as medicine. And in *Laddie* the hero—who was modeled after her beloved older brother Leander—cheerfully drives a reaper and hoes corn on a farm identical to the one on which Stratton-Porter was raised.

"I live in the country and work in the woods," Stratton-Porter once wrote, "so no other location is possible for my backgrounds, and only the people with whom I come in daily contact there are suitable for my actors."

Unlike some other writers of that era, among them the Hoosier novelist Theodore Dreiser, Stratton-Porter avoided writing about the dark side of human nature or life's harsh realities. In her novels "good" people faced obstacles and had their share of problems. But as a result of their determination, hard work, and decency, they overcame hurdles and lived happily ever-after. As one modern-day literary critic noted, Stratton-Porter continually sketched "an America without tears." In her fictional world, bad people were punished and honorable people were rewarded; goodness always prevailed over evil.

Unable to accept her "sugary" vision of life, the literary critics of Stratton-Porter's era openly scorned her fiction. They, as well as some readers, denounced it as overly sweet and unrealistic. "Her books are childish and they insult the adult intelligence," said one critic. A minister complained that "her novels are nothing but molasses fiction." But to all who picked apart her work, Stratton-Porter replied, "Now what do I care for the newspaper or magazine critic yammering that . . . my pictures of life are sentimental and idealized. They are! And I glory in them!"

"To my way of thinking and working," she added on more than one occasion, "the greatest service a piece of fiction can do any reader is to force him to lay it down with a higher ideal of life than he had when he took it up. If in one small degree it shows him where he can be a gentler, saner, cleaner, kinder man, it is a wonder-working book."

Though not the best-sellers that her novels were, Stratton-Porter's nonfiction books still were popular. Readers appreciated what scholarly critics did not: Stratton-Porter wrote about birds and wildlife in a way that most people could understand, without pages of footnotes, confusing statistics, and unpronounceable scientific words. Her nature books, which she illustrated with her own photographs, represented years of field work and study—enough, she believed, to rival that of any scientist. Her books also reflected her total devotion to her work. To produce *Moths of the Limberlost*, she brought cocoons home from the woods, hung them among the flowers in her conservatory, and then proceeded to raise her own specimens. She even went so far as to pin cocoons close to her pillow at night so she would be awakened by the scraping of feet when the moths—"these fragile night wanderers, these moonflowers of June's darkness"—emerged.

Stratton-Porter's worship of all living things led many Americans to do exactly what the author hoped: They left their front porches to clamber down riverbanks, explore woods and fields, and poke around in swamp grass. They also began thinking in new ways about their relationship with wild creatures and wild places. "Tens of thousands of people," Stratton-Porter wrote midway in her career, "have sent me word that directly through my works they have been led outdoors and to a higher conception of the beauties of Nature. My mail brings an average of ten such letters a day from students and teachers." Other observers, impressed by her large following, didn't dispute those numbers. "I have no doubt," remarked the educator William Lyon Phelps, "that she has led millions of boys and girls into the study of natural objects."

But even when Stratton-Porter's books didn't inspire readers to hunt for luna moths, transplant bittersweet, or listen for the sweet song of a wood thrush, they still informed and entertained. And at the height of Stratton-Porter's popularity in 1918, the novelist Grant Overton summed up how extraordinarily influential she was:

> Let no one underestimate the tremendous power that is hers . . . let no one underestimate her hold upon millions of readers; let none undervalue the influence she has exerted and continues to exert, an influence always for good, for clean living . . . for love of nature.

* * *

By 1913 Stratton-Porter's beloved Limberlost was disappearing. Developers who wanted the swamp's timber, oil, and gas resources had begun draining the land, clearing the trees, and permitting farmers to plant fields of onions, celery, and sugar beets. For Stratton-Porter all the dredging, ditching, and road-building made it impossible to continue her fieldwork. Left with few alternatives, she moved.

Her new outdoor laboratory was on Sylvan Lake near Rome City, where she had met Charles years earlier. With money earned from the sales of her books, she bought a hundred and twenty acres at the south end the lake, an area marked by deep valleys, thick forest, and winding roadways. Not far from the shore, in the midst of beech, tulip, and oak trees, she built a large home modeled after her cedar-log cabin in Geneva. She called it Limberlost North.

She was immensely fond of her new retreat, and when not writing and photographing, she worked tirelessly to make it a wildlife sanctuary. She arranged for diseased and damaged trees to be cleared away, leaving room for healthy timber to attract birds. She journeyed to swamps and woodlands around the region, where she collected flowers and plants threatened

"IN THE OLD DAYS when we did field work together, I have seen her stop the horse, clamber down from the buggy, and straighten a wild flower, broken by some careless foot, put the dirt around it, prop it up with a stick or stone, straighten the petals and leaves carefully, and give it a drink from her thermos bottle."

— as recalled by her daughter Jeannette Porter Meehan

with extinction. The transplanted specimens—orchids, arrow-head lilies, rosemary, ferns, and others—soon flourished on her property, leading Stratton-Porter to name her estate "Wildflower Woods." As more and more people learned about her efforts to save "these delicate little blossoms," admirers began sending her seeds and rare plants from around the world. Eventually more than seventeen thousand flowers, vines, shrubs, and trees were introduced to Wildflower Woods, with Stratton-Porter planting most of them herself.

She had fully intended, after devoting so much time and energy to her new home, to spend the rest of her life along that "exquisitely beautiful strip of lake shore." She even picked out the place on her estate where she wished to be buried. But in 1919, after suffering a serious bout with the flu, she traveled to California to rest and to enjoy a warmer climate. Once there, she found the weather to be ideal— "I love being out all year around"—and she was deeply moved by the beauty of the mountains, desert, canyons, and ocean. She returned to Wildflower Woods in the spring but soon was dividing her time between there and the West Coast. By 1923, she had decided to live year-round in California. She bought property on a small mountain near Los Angeles, with plans to build a new home and workshop there. And on nearby Catalina Island, where seals played on the rocks and wild goats bleated atop cliffs, she built a vacation retreat.

Always an intensely private person, Stratton-Porter began socializing more in California, though without the companionship of Charles. Nearly seventy years old when his wife moved west, Charles remained in Indiana, where he continued to look after his business affairs (he visited her there in the winter, however). The couple's daughter Jeannette, who was divorced by then and raising two young daughters, joined her mother in Los Angeles in late 1920. Jeannette would later write that her mother found the city to be a "very delightful, restful spot." To friends back in Indiana Stratton-Porter herself wrote that "next to the sunshine" what she liked most

about California was meeting "actors, poets, authors, paint-
ers, sculptors, from all over the world."

"Fine folk these artistic and creative people be!" she declared in a Christmas letter to her Hoosier friends. "Some of
them are self-seeking and selfish and pushing, as is the manner of humanity; but most of them are world-experienced,
educated in adversity, a real treat."

Among those Stratton-Porter came to know were Hollywood filmmakers, who urged her to let them make her books
into movies. (That was still the silent-film era.) She wasn't
interested, largely because a few years earlier she had permitted a film company to produce her novel *Freckles* and was
unhappy with the results. She was intrigued, however, by the
idea of making her own movies—ones that would faithfully
represent her books and emphasize wholesome family entertainment. With her usual strong will and determination, she
organized Gene Stratton-Porter Productions, hired a young
director, and went into business. Her films were not smash
hits, but they drew big enough crowds to convince her that
moviegoers wanted something other than sex and violence on
screen. Very quickly she became an outspoken advocate for
decency in movies and began urging parents, educators, and
church members to join her in lobbying the film industry for
"better pictures."

"When you stop to consider," she wrote to the president of
a women's organization, "that picture making is the third
largest industry in the United States to-day and that a bad
picture reaches more people than any other one medium,
certainly it is worth while for the women who are trying to
better conditions to take hold of the picture question . . ."

When not involved in her film work, Stratton-Porter continued to write novels, though her popularity as a storyteller
was beginning to decline. Novels such as *Her Father's Daughter* (1921) and *The White Flag* (1923) weren't the top sellers
that her earlier books had been. Still, Stratton-Porter didn't
have time to worry. She began experimenting with poetry. She

also began writing essays for magazines, and as a result of her monthly column in *McCall's*, she developed a new following of loyal readers—most of them middle-class American housewives who appreciated her advice on everything from gardening to how to grow old gracefully.

Beyond that, Stratton-Porter continued to promote wildlife conservation, both with her pen and in person. In various magazine articles and in her nature books, she pleaded for the protection of birds: wood ducks, passenger pigeons, wild turkeys, owls. She urged for an end to the widespread destruction of forests to create farmland. She condemned people who out of greed and recklessness killed more fish and animals than they needed. And she warned that draining wetlands would adversely affect rainfall patterns and alter climate.

In a 1922 editorial that was typical of her work—and that appeared on the cover of the magazine *Outdoor America*—she issued this rallying cry for land conservation:

> If we do not want our land to dry up and blow away, we must replace at least part of our lost trees. We must save every brook and stream and lake . . . and those of us who see the vision and most keenly feel the need must furnish the motor power for those less responsive. Work must be done. It is the time for all of us to get together and in unison make a test of our strength. All together, Heave!

* * *

Blessed with good health and abundant energy, Stratton-Porter showed few signs of slowing down in 1924, the year she turned sixty-one. Along with managing her film company and supervising construction on her Los Angeles home, she completed her twelfth novel, *The Keeper of the Bees*, in record time. But on the evening of December 6, 1924, her limousine collided with a streetcar less than a block from her home. The impact threw her from the vehicle and left her unconscious. She was rushed by ambulance to a nearby hospital. Less than two hours later she died.

Fiercely proud of her work, Stratton-Porter always wanted to be remembered as a great writer. Toward the end of her life, she had grown "desperately tired" of critics who judged her fiction harshly, and she was sure that eventually they would be proved wrong. "Time, the hearts of my readers, and the files of my publishers," she once wrote, "will find me my ultimate place."

Whatever her "ultimate" place in history, Stratton-Porter is remembered today as a woman who dared to develop her own interests and talents at a time when women were supposed to concern themselves solely with their families and homes. She is also remembered as a writer who keenly observed the outdoor world, and who, through her many books and articles, taught people from all walks of life how to appreciate the bugs and blossoms around them.

Beyond that, she is admired by many for being among the first Americans to issue an environmental wake-up cry. Long before it was fashionable to talk about saving the planet, Stratton-Porter correctly warned that our natural resources must be protected or, failing that, we would suffer grave consequences.

Those today who study the life of this novelist, nature writer, naturalist, and photographer find no shortage of material to review and reflect upon. If Stratton-Porter had had her way, she eagerly would have supplied modern readers with more.

"If I had a hundred years to live and strength to write a book for every one of them," she once wrote, "I could fill them all cram full of comparatively new, interesting things, from everyday life about me."

SUGGESTIONS FOR FURTHER READING

Finney, Jan Dearmin. *Gene Stratton-Porter: The Natural Wonder*. Mattituck, N.Y.: Amereon Ltd., 1983.

King, Rollin Patterson. *Gene Stratton-Porter: A Lovely Light*. Chicago: Adams Press, 1979.

Long, Judith Reick. *Gene Stratton-Porter: Novelist and Naturalist*. Indianapolis: Indiana Historical Society, 1990.

MacLean, David G., editor. *Gene Stratton-Porter Remembered . . . Reprints of Selected Articles*. Decatur, Ind.: Americana Books, 1987, first booklet of series; 1990, booklets two through six.

Meehan, Jeannette Porter. *Life and Letters of Gene Stratton-Porter*. Garden City, N.Y.: Doubleday, Doran & Company, 1928, reprinted, Kennikat Press, 1972.

Richards, Bertrand F. *Gene Stratton Porter*. Boston: Twayne Publishers, 1980.

S.F.E., compiler. *Gene Stratton-Porter: A Little Story of the Life and Work and Ideals of "The Bird Woman."* Garden City, N.Y.: Doubleday, Page & Company, 1915. This booklet, identified only by the initials, S.F.E., is assumed to have been written by Eugene Francis Saxton and/or Samuel F. Ewart.

106

At the edge of the Limberlost.

IT WAS THOREAU who, in writing of the destruction of the forests, exclaimed, "Thank Heaven, they can not cut down the clouds!" Aye, but they can! That is a miserable fact, and soon it will become our discomfort and loss. Clouds are beds of vapor arising from damp places . . . If men in their greed cut forests that preserve and distil moisture, clear fields, take the shelter of trees from creeks and rivers until they evaporate, and drain the water from swamps so that they can be cleared and cultivated, — they *prevent vapor from rising*; and if it does not rise it can not fall. Pity of pities it is; but man can change and is changing the forces of nature. I never told a sadder truth, but it is truth that man can "cut down the clouds."

—*Music of the Wild*, 1912

Photo by Gene Stratton-Porter

A Girl of the Limberlost

(from Chapter 1)

"Elnora Comstock, have you lost your senses?" demanded the angry voice of Katharine Comstock as she glared at her daughter.

"Why, Mother?" faltered the girl.

"Don't you 'why mother' me!" cried Mrs. Comstock. "You know very well what I mean. You've given me no peace until you've had your way about this going to school business; I've fixed you good enough, and you're ready to start. But no child of mine walks the streets of Onabasha looking like a play-actress woman. You wet your hair and comb it down modest and decent and then be off, or you'll have no time to find where you belong."

Elnora gave one despairing glance at the white face, framed in a most becoming riot of reddish-brown hair, which she saw in the little kitchen mirror. Then she untied the narrow black ribbon, wet the comb and plastered the waving curls close to her head, bound them fast, pinned on the skimpy black hat and started for the back door.

"You've gone so plum daffy you are forgetting your dinner," jeered her mother.

"I don't want anything to eat," replied Elnora without stopping.

"You'll take your dinner or you'll not go one step. Are you crazy? Walk nearly three miles and no food from six in the morning until six at night. A pretty figure you'd cut if you had your way about things! And after I've gone and bought you this nice new pail and filled it especial for the first day!"

Elnora came back with a face still whiter and picked up the lunch. "Thank you, mother! Good-bye!" she said. Mrs. Comstock did not reply. She watched the girl down the long walk to the gate and out of sight on the road in the bright sunshine of the first Monday of September.

"I bet a dollar she gets enough of it by night!" Mrs. Comstock said positively.

Elnora walked by instinct for her eyes were blinded with tears. She left the road where it turned south at the corner of the Limberlost, climbed a snake fence and entered a path worn by her own feet. Dodging under willow and scrub oak branches she at last came to the faint outline of an old trail made in the days when the precious timber of the swamp was guarded by armed men. This path she followed until she reached a thick clump of bushes. From the debris in the end of a hollow log she took a key that unlocked the padlock of a large weatherbeaten old box, inside of which lay several books, a butterfly apparatus, and an old cracked mirror. The walls were lined thickly with gaudy butterflies, dragon-flies, and moths. She set up the mirror, and once more pulling the ribbon from her hair, she shook the bright mass over her shoulders, tossing it dry in the sunshine. Then she straightened it, bound it loosely, and replaced her hat. She tugged vainly at the low brown calico collar and gazed despairingly at the generous length of the narrow skirt. She lifted it as she would have liked it to be cut if possible. That disclosed the heavy leather high shoes, at sight of which she looked positively ill, and hastily dropped the skirt. She opened the pail, took out the lunch, wrapped it in the napkin, and placed it in a small pasteboard box. Locking the case again she hid the key and hurried down the trail.

She followed it around the north end of the swamp and then struck into a footpath crossing a farm in the direction of the spires of the city to the northeast. Again she climbed a fence and was on the open road. For an instant she leaned against the fence staring before her, then turned and looked back. Behind her lay the land on which she had been born to drudgery and a mother who made no pretence of loving her; before her lay the city through whose schools she hoped to find means of escape and the way to reach the things for which she cared. When she thought of how she looked she leaned more heavily against the fence and groaned; when she thought of turning back and wearing such clothing in ignorance all the days of her life, she set her teeth firmly and went hastily toward Onabasha.

At the bridge crossing a deep culvert at the suburbs she glanced around, and then kneeling she thrust the lunch box between the foundation and the flooring. This left her empty-handed as she approached the great stone high school building. She entered bravely and inquired her way to the office of the superintendent. There she learned that she should have come the week before and arranged for her classes. There were many things incident to the opening of school, and one man unable to cope with all of them.

"Where have you been attending school?" he asked, as he advised the teacher of the cooking department not to telephone for groceries until she saw how many she would have in her classes; wrote an order for chemicals for the students of science; and advised the leader of the orchestra to try to get a professional to take the place of the bass violist, reported suddenly ill.

"I finished last spring at Brushwood school, district number nine," said Elnora. "I have been studying all summer. I am quite sure I can do the first year work, if I have a few days to get started."

"Of course, of course," assented the superintendent. "Almost invariably country pupils do good work. You may enter first year, and if you don't fit, we will find it out speedily. Your teachers will tell you the list of books you must have, and if you will come with me I will show you the way to the auditorium. It is now time for opening exercises. Take any seat you find vacant." He was gone. . . .

When the hour was gone the class filed back to the study room and Elnora followed in desperation, because she did not know where else to go. She could not study as she had no books, and when the class again left the room to go to another professor for the next recitation, she went also. At least they could put her out if she did not belong there. Noon came at last, and she kept with the others until they dispersed on the sidewalk. She was so abnormally self conscious she fancied all the hundreds of that laughing throng saw and jested at her. When she passed the brown-eyed boy walking with the girl of her encounter she knew, for she heard him say, "Did you really let that gawky piece of calico get ahead of you?" The answer was indistinct.

Elnora hurried from the city. She intended to get her lunch, eat it in the shade of the first tree, and then decide whether she would go back or go home. She knelt on the bridge and reached for her box, but it was so very light that she was prepared for the fact that it was empty before opening it. There was just one thing for which to be thankful. The boy or tramp who had seen her hide it, had left the napkin. She would not have to face her mother and account for its loss. She put it in her pocket, and threw the box into the ditch. Then she sat on the bridge and tried to think, but her brain was confused.

"Perhaps the worst is over," she said at last. "I will go back. What would mother say to me if I came home now?"

So she returned to the high school, followed some other pupils to the coat room, hung her hat, and found her way to the study where she had been in the morning. Twice that afternoon, with aching head and empty stomach, she faced strange professors, in different branches. Once she escaped notice, the second time the worst happened. She was asked a question she could not answer.

"Have you not decided on your course, and secured your books?" inquired the professor.

"I have decided on my course," replied Elnora, "I do not know who to ask for my books."

"Ask?" the professor was bewildered.

"I understood the books were furnished," faltered Elnora.

"Only to those bringing an order from the township trustee," replied the Professor.

"No! Oh, no!" cried Elnora. "I will get them tomorrow," and gripped her desk for support for she knew that was not true. Four books, ranging perhaps at a dollar and a half apiece; would her mother get them? Of course she would not—could not.

Did not Elnora know the story by heart. There was enough land, but no one to do clearing and farm. Tax on all those acres, recently the new gravel road tax added, the expense of living and only the work of two women to meet all of it. She was insane to think she could come to the city to school. Her mother had been right. The girl decided that if only she lived to get home, she would stay there and lead any sort of life to avoid more of this torture. Bad as what she wished to escape had been, it was nothing like this. She never could live down the movement that went through the class when she inadvertently revealed the fact that she had expected her books to be furnished. Her mother would not get them; that settled the question.

But the end of misery is never in a hurry to come, for before the day was over the superintendent entered the room and explained that pupils from the country were charged a tuition of twenty dollars a year. That really was the end. Previously Elnora had canvassed a dozen wild plans for securing the money for books, ranging all the way from offering to wash the superintendent's dishes to breaking into the bank. The additional expense made the thing so wildly impossible, there was nothing to do but hold up her head until she was out of sight.

Down the long corridor alone among hundreds, down the long street alone among thousands, out into the country she came at last. Across the fence and field, along the old trail once trodden by a boy's bitter agony, now stumbled a white-faced girl, sick at heart. She sat on a log and began to sob in spite of her efforts at self-control. At first it was physical breakdown, later, thought came crowding.

Oh, the shame, the mortification! Why had she not known of the tuition? How did she happen to think that in the city books were furnished? Perhaps it was because she had read they were in several states. But why did she not know? Why did not her mother go with her? Other mothers—but when had her mother ever been or done anything at all like other mothers? Because she never had been it was useless to blame her now. Elnora felt she should have gone to town the week before, called on some one and learned all these things herself. She should have remembered how her clothing would look, before she wore it in public places. Now she knew, and her dreams were over. She must go home to feed chickens, calves, and pigs, wear calico and coarse shoes, and pass a library with averted head all her life. She sobbed again.

"For pity's sake, honey, what's the matter?" asked the voice of the nearest neighbour, Wesley Sinton, as he seated himself by Elnora. "There, there," he continued, smearing tears all over her face in an effort to dry them. "Was it so bad as that, now? Maggie has been just about wild over you all day. She's got nervouser every minute. She said we were foolish to let you go. She said your clothes were not right, you ought not to carry that tin pail, and that they would laugh at you. By gum, I see they did!"

"Oh, Uncle Wesley," sobbed the girl, "why didn't she tell me?"

"Well, you see, Elnora, she didn't like to. You got such a way of holding up your head, and going through with things. She thought someway that you'd make it, till you got started, and then she begun to see a hundred things we should have done. I reckon you hadn't reached that building before she remembered that your skirt should have been pleated instead of gathered, your shoes been low, and lighter for hot September weather, and a new hat. Were your things right, Elnora?"

The girl broke into hysterical laughter. "Right!" she cried. "Right! Uncle Wesley, you should have seen me among them! I was a picture! They'll never forget me. No, they won't get the chance, for they'll see the same things to-morrow!"

"Now, that is what I call spunk, Elnora! Downright grit," said Wesley Sinton. "Don't you let them laugh you out. You've helped Margaret and me for years at harvest and busy times; what you've earned must amount to quite a sum. You can get yourself a good many clothes with it."

"Don't mention clothes, Uncle Wesley," sobbed Elnora. "I don't care now how I look. If I don't go back all of them will know it's because I am so poor I can't buy my books."

"Oh, I don't know as you are so dratted poor," said Sinton meditatively. "There are three hundred acres of good land, with fine timber as ever grew on it."

"It takes all we can earn to pay the tax, and mother wouldn't cut a tree for her life."

"Well, then, maybe, I'll be compelled to cut one for her," suggested Sinton. "Anyway, stop tearing yourself to pieces and tell me. If it isn't clothes, what is it?"

"It's books and tuition. Over twenty dollars in all."

"Humph! First time I ever knew you to be stumped by twenty dollars, Elnora," said Sinton, patting her hand.

"It's the first time you ever knew me to want money," answered Elnora. "This is different from anything that ever happened to me. Oh, how can I get it, Uncle Wesley?"

"Drive to town with me in the morning and I'll draw it from the bank for you. I owe you every cent of it."

"You know you don't owe me a penny, and I wouldn't touch one from you, unless I really could earn it. For anything that's past I owe you and Aunt Margaret for all the home life and love I've ever known. I know how you work, and I'll not take your money."

"Just a loan, Elnora, just a loan for a little while until you can earn it. You can be proud with all the rest of the world, but there's no secrets between us, is there, Elnora?"

"No," said Elnora, "there are none. You and Aunt Margaret have given me all the love there has been in my life. That is the one reason above all others why you shall not give me charity. Hand me money because you find me crying for it! This isn't the first time this old trail has known tears and heartache. All of us know that story. Freckles stuck to what he undertook and won out. I stick, too. When Duncan moved away he gave me all Freckles left in the swamp, and as I have inherited his property maybe his luck will come with it. I won't touch your money, but I'll win some way. First, I'm going home and try mother. It's just possible I could find second-hand books, and perhaps all the tuition need not be paid at once. Maybe they would accept it quarterly. But, oh, Uncle Wesley, you and Aunt Margaret keep on loving me! I'm so lonely, and no one else cares!". . .

"There's one thing you don't consider, Elnora," said the man earnestly. "And that's what you are to Maggie. She's a little like your ma. She hasn't given up to it, and she's struggling on brave, but when we buried our second little girl the light went out of Maggie's eyes, and it's not come back. The only time I ever see a hint of it is when she thinks she's done something that makes you happy, Elnora. Now, you go easy about refusing her anything she wants to do for you. There's times in this world when it's our bounden duty to forget ourselves, and think what will help other people. Young woman, you owe me and Maggie all the comfort we can get out of you. There's the two of our own we can't ever do anything for. Don't you get the idea into your head that a fool thing you call pride, is going to cut us out of all the pleasure we have in life beside ourselves."

"Uncle Wesley, you are a dear," said Elnora. "Just a dear! If I can't possibly get that money any way else on earth, I'll come and borrow it of you, and then I'll pay it back if I dig ferns from the swamp and sell them from door to door in the city. I'll even plant them, so that they will be sure to come up in the spring. I have been sort of panic stricken all day and couldn't think. I can gather nuts and sell them. Freckles sold moths and butterflies, and I've a lot collected. Of course, I am going back to-morrow! I can find a way to get the books. Don't you worry about me. I am all right!"

"SHE IS AS FULL of energy as Theodore Roosevelt, and as hearty an American."

When William Lyon Phelps, a prominent educator and literary critic, made that remark in the early 1900s, he wasn't the first person to compare Gene Stratton-Porter to President Roosevelt. Both the "Bird Woman" from Indiana and the politician from New York loved the outdoors. And both helped teach Americans about the importance of preserving natural resources.

Roosevelt developed his passion for wide, open spaces during the 1880s, when he interrupted his political career briefly to run two cattle ranches in the Dakota Territory. He returned to his home in New York in 1886. But he regularly took vacations in the West, and with each trip he was increasingly disturbed by what he saw. Loggers were carelessly cutting down forests. Hunters were needlessly slaughtering buffalo, elk, and other animals. Mining operators were damaging land and wasting minerals with their sloppy and greedy practices.

Determined to save what was left of the "wild West," Roosevelt helped organize a club dedicated to preserving wilderness areas. Known as the Boone and Crockett Club, that conservation group was successful in getting Congress to take proper care of Yellowstone National Park in Wyoming. The club also worked successfully for legislation to protect sequoia trees in California. And it promoted other measures to keep large areas of the West free from development.

As governor of New York in the late 1890s, Roosevelt continued to work for conservation. He spoke against the polluting of Adirondack streams and supported laws to protect birds. When he reached the White House in 1901, he took even bolder steps. He established five national parks, added about 150 million acres to the national forests, and created the first fifty-five bird and game preserves. He also designated eighteen sites, including the Grand Canyon, as the first national monuments. By the time he left office in 1909, he was known

as the "Conservation President."

Roosevelt and Stratton-Porter admired each other, enough that the President once invited the Hoosier naturalist to spend an afternoon at his Sagamore Hill home on Long Island, New York. Although each came from different backgrounds and pursued different careers, they shared a common belief —namely, that America did not have an endless supply of land, forests, wildlife, and clean air and water. Working tirelessly to awaken people to that viewpoint, neither Roosevelt nor Stratton-Porter changed public opinion overnight. But their passionate pleas for protection of natural resources started people thinking in fresh ways about the environment—and prodded many Americans into action.

"Each has swayed the millions," the author Grant Overton wrote of Roosevelt and Stratton-Porter in the 1920s. "Each, beyond all possible question, has influenced human lives. Neither was oppressed by the enormous responsibility attached to such a role."

BOTH OF THE HOMES Gene Stratton-Porter built in Indiana have been designated state historic sites.

The Limberlost Cabin on the outskirts of the village of Geneva was much admired by local townsfolk when it was finished in 1895. Designed by Gene and her husband Charles, the two-story house was built using Wisconsin cedar logs and redwood shingles. The rustic architecture was inspired by the Forestry Building that the Porters saw while visiting the World's Columbian Exposition in Chicago in 1893.

Inside the cabin are fourteen rooms, including the conservatory where Gene grew tulips, hyacinths, and daffodils. Among items on display in the home are Gene's bed with its owl carvings on the headboard and a moth collection which she mounted in 1906.

The Cabin in the Wildflower Woods, which Gene began building in 1913 after the Limberlost Swamp was drained, lies on the shores of Sylvan Lake near Rome City. This two-story home of Wisconsin cedar logs is a larger version of the Limberlost Cabin. Its special features include cherry paneling in the entrance hall and dining room. There are also four fireplaces, two of which—in Gene's words—"I practically built myself."

Behind the home visitors can enjoy the beauty of Gene's lush gardens, arbor, and orchard. They can also wander scenic paths through woods that provided rich material for Gene's nature studies and photography—woods still filled with clumps of pokeberry bushes, stands of beech and tulip trees, and patches of goldenrod, aster, and wild ginger. Today the historic site encompasses twenty of the property's original one hundred and fifty acres.

Photo by Gene Stratton-Porter

(Top) The Limberlost Cabin at Geneva, Indiana. (Center) Stratton-Porter's home at Wildflower Woods. (Left) The grape arbor at Wildflower Woods.

Center and lower photos courtesy Gene Stratton-Porter Historic Site, Indiana State Museum

THE MARSH

... there were miles of unbroken forest... Then the Winter Swamp had all the lacy exquisite beauty of such locations when snow and frost draped, while from May until October it was practically tropical jungle.

—*Moths of the Limberlost*, 1912

RAINBOW BOTTOM

Scattered around were mighty trees, but conspicuous above any, in the very center, was a giant sycamore, split at its base into three large trees, whose waving branches seemed to sweep the face of heaven, and whose roots, like miserly fingers, clutched deep into the black muck of Rainbow Bottom.

—*The Song of the Cardinal*, 1903

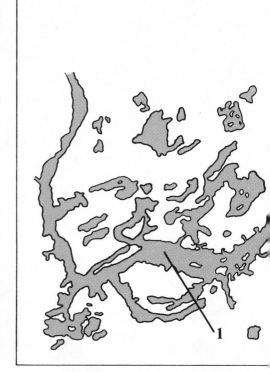

BLACK VULTURE NEST

... there were steaming, fetid pools everywhere, swarms of flies, gnats, mosquitoes, and poisonous insects, masses of poisonous vines and at every step not only the ground but the bushes about, had to be watched for rattlesnakes. The muck was so spongy we sank ankle-deep, bushes scratched and tore at us and logs we thought were solid let us down knee-deep.

—*What I Have Done With Birds*, 1907

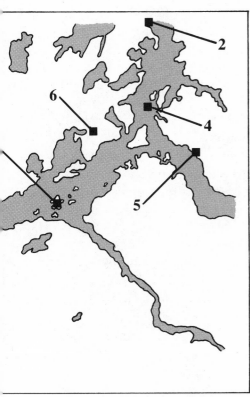

Map courtesy of Ken Brunswick.

1. THE MARSH
2. RAINBOW BOTTOM
3. BLACK VULTURE NEST
4. VALLEY OF THE WOOD ROBIN
5. RIVERSIDE CEMETERY
6. THE LIMBERLOST CABIN

VALLEY OF THE WOOD ROBIN

[There] . . . grew giant forest trees and almost impenetrable thickets of underbrush. There were masses of dogwood, hawthorn, wild plum, ironwood and wild rose bushes . . . grape-vines, trumpet creeper and wild ivy clambered everywhere, while the ground was covered with violets, anemones, spring beauties, cowslips, and many varieties of mosses and ferns.

—*Friends in Feathers*, 1917

RIVERSIDE CEMETERY

The clover field . . . stood high and dry, spreading beside the road for a long stretch . . . all day long the river sang as it lovingly circled around it giving it living waters; . . . Myriads of birds . . . sang their courting songs, builded their nests, and reared their young there . . . Among those who lie beside the winding roadway . . . daily visited by the birds descended from those I worked among, rest many who were my best friends.

—*Tales You Won't Believe*, 1925

THE LIMBERLOST SWAMP that Gene Stratton-Porter so vividly described in her writings once covered approximately twenty-five thousand acres in Adams, Jay, and Wells counties in northeastern Indiana. In her day, it encompassed wetlands, grassy marshes, narrow lakes, small islands, and dense woods stocked with majestic elms, oaks, sycamores, willows, and cottonwoods. A state geologist's report in 1881 stated that the region abounded in rare plants and that "its beautiful orchids, gigantic grasses, sedges and ferns, make it a botanist's paradise."

Long ago a retreating glacier cut a river channel through the region, paving the way for creation of the swamp. Over the years, the river's bed gradually filled with decaying plants and animals. The more the dead vegetation piled up, the more shallow the river water became. As trees grew taller and vegetation grew thicker, the shallow water moved even more sluggishly toward the Wabash River. Eventually the swamp was born.

Local Indians referred to the swamp as the Loblolly, which roughly translated meant "stinking water." Legends say the name Limberlost came from an early pioneer named either Jim Corbus or Jimmy McDowel. According to one legend, the pioneer was nicknamed "Limber Jim" because he was thin and wiry. According to another legend, he was a limber dancer at hoedowns. Sometime between 1820 and 1838 "Limber Jim" became lost in the swamp, leading people to refer to the area as Limber's Lost—or Limberlost—Swamp.

In the late 1800s, businessmen saw a chance to profit from the timber, oil, and natural gas within the Limberlost. To reach these valuable resources, work crews started draining the swamp in 1888, with dredging continuing into the early 1900s. In 1913 crews resumed their work, digging ditches even deeper. By then, Stratton-Porter had decided she could no longer bear to watch the swamp being destroyed. She left the area for a new home and outdoor laboratory on Sylvan Lake near Rome City.

Today some people, through a project known as Limberlost Swamp Remembered, are trying to restore a portion of the former swamp to its wild state. Organizers would like to convert a few hundred acres, much of it now farmland, into wetlands and create a nature preserve. They hope that schoolchildren can someday hike through marshy fields and woods to see some of the natural wonders that Stratton-Porter photographed and described. They also hope to offer educational programs about the area's history and instruct visitors on the important role wetlands play in the environment.

Though it's likely to take decades to convert the Limberlost back to its natural state, some local landowners are helping by no longer farming their acreage. Already hundreds of waterfowl—mallards, bufflehead, green-winged teal, mergansers, wood ducks—have returned to the newly restored wetlands.

Plants not seen for years also are making a comeback. At the fringes of shallow ponds are thick growths of cattails, bulrushes, horsetails, swamp milkweed, chicory, ironweed, and thistle.

"The Limberlost stirred . . ." wrote Gene Stratton-Porter in 1904 in her best-selling novel *Freckles*. Today, in a small part of Limberlost country, the swamp is stirring again.

124

(Above) Stratton-Porter and her granddaughter Jeannette Helen, to whom she dedicated *Morning Face*, a book of children's nature verse. (Left) Stratton-Porter, the naturalist, brushing the wing of a butterfly at Wildflower Woods.

Stratton-Porter and her touring car loaded with plants collected on one of her many field trips.

(Below) Stratton-Porter with her daughter Jeannette and son-in-law James Leo Meehan, who directed her movies. (Right) Charles Dorwin Porter in California in 1923.

Left and lower photos courtesy Gene Stratton-Porter Historic Site, Indiana State Museum

Courtesy Geneva Public Library

The cast who appeared in *The Harvester*, which was filmed at Wildflower Woods in 1927.

126

Stratton-Porter on a
California beach,
patiently waiting to
feed her featherd
friends—and then
joining her family.

Photos by Gene Stratton-Porter

Bluebird eating a worm for breakfast.

"Little Chicken," the black vulture that Stratton-Porter and Charles discovered in a hollow tree deep within the Limberlost.

Hickory Moth.

Lady Slippers.

Booth Tarkington

4

BOOTH TARKINGTON

ONE DAY WHILE READING aloud a chapter he had just written, the Hoosier novelist Booth Tarkington began laughing so hard that his wife urged him to control himself.

"I'm not laughing at what I've written," he replied. "I'm laughing at how funny boys are."

Writing about boys was a specialty of Tarkington's. Unlike other authors, who typically portrayed children in fiction as either all good or all bad, Tarkington wrote about boys as they really are: loud and lovable, selfish and sensitive, crude and clever. He drew upon his own experiences growing up in Indianapolis in the late nineteenth century to create his "true-boy" characters. And when memories of his youth were fuzzy, he looked for inspiration to his three nephews and their chums, whose escapades in his neighborhood constantly amused him.

The most famous of all Tarkington's boy creations was Penrod Schofield, that twelve-year-old rascal who first charmed audiences in 1913. The world is far different now than it was at the turn of the century, when Penrod suffered through Friday Afternoon Dancing Class, dipped the end of a girl's braid in the inkwell, threw his arithmetic book down the cistern, and went looking for adventure with his wistful dog Duke. Even so, the Penrod stories continue to delight new generations of readers. And modern youngsters find that, despite the changing times, they share common frustrations and fantasies with Penrod—especially when he encounters boring teachers, humorless adults, fat-faced bullies, and a snobbish girl with amber curls.

By the time Tarkington died in 1946, he had grown rich and famous from the *Penrod* books. But his reputation as a gifted writer wasn't based solely on his tales of boyhood life. During a literary career that spanned nearly fifty years, Tarkington wrote forty-one novels and short-story collections, twenty-three plays, and dozens of articles and essays. Nearly everything he wrote was popular, and his fans eagerly looked forward to his next book. Two of his most admired novels— *The Magnificent Ambersons* and *Alice Adams*—dealt with economic and social changes taking place in America around the turn of the century. Both of these serious studies earned him the coveted Pulitzer Prize in fiction.

Revered in his home state, and especially in his home city of Indianapolis, Tarkington was everything Hoosiers wanted in their writers. He was well-educated, warmhearted, and witty. He was interested in people, especially the American middle class about which he wrote so perceptively. And he was a man who always emphasized "good taste" in literature. Unlike his contemporary, the Indiana-born novelist Theodore Dreiser, Tarkington didn't shock readers with stories marked by grimy realism or dark cynicism. Instead, he wrote tales that were wholesome and pleasant. And while he didn't shy away from criticizing society, he did so without bitterness and usually with gentle humor. Always he wrote in a form and style that readers could understand.

"Tarkington did not always write great books, but he always wrote good ones," observed the Hoosier author and publisher R. E. Banta many years ago. "Probably, as time goes on, it will be realized increasingly that the best of his efforts are important social documents, that the lightest of them have a Mark Twain quality of surviving freshness and that they are all good entertainment."

* * *

Newton Booth Tarkington, like his fictional Penrod Schofield, grew up in a closely knit family that was well liked and respected. Booth's father, John Stevenson Tarkington, was an attorney who early in his career served in the Indiana legislature. During the Civil War he joined the Union Army as an infantry captain, and when the fighting ended he served briefly as a circuit court judge. Known for his generosity and kindness, John Tarkington passed his gentle nature on to Booth. When the elder Tarkington died at age ninety, Booth wrote to a friend that his father had been "always & always the blessing of the lives of all his family."

Tarkington's mother was Elizabeth Booth, a descendant of the first settlers of Connecticut. Born and reared in Indiana, she was better educated than many women of that era. Her father, an independent-minded Presbyterian, had arranged for her to attend St. Mary of the Woods, a Catholic institution which at the time was the best school in her home town of Terre Haute. As a result of her schooling and upbringing, the proud and ambitious Elizabeth brought refinement to the Tarkington household. In both Booth and his older sister Haute, Elizabeth instilled a love of the arts.

Booth was born on July 29, 1869, four years after the end of the Civil War. His birthplace, Indianapolis, was not yet the smoky, dirty industrialized city he would later write about in his novels. In the 1870s and 1880s it was still a small neighborly community where homes were shaded by trees left from wilderness days, where carriages and mule-drawn streetcars traveled leisurely along uncongested avenues, and where men in bowler hats and women in long silk dresses moved at an unhurried pace.

When Booth was four, hard economic times caused his father's law practice to suffer. With money scarce, the Tarkingtons moved from their comfortable home on Meridian Street to a less attractive neighborhood on New York Street. Within a few years, however, John Tarkington's law practice revived. By the time Booth was eight, his family moved into a tall brick house at 1100 North Pennsylvania Street on Indianapolis' fashionable north side, where families hired coachmen to groom their horses and immigrant "girls" to cook. Booth lived in that house, with its dark woodwork, high ceilings and Victorian furnishings, on and off for the next forty-six years. When he finally moved to another part of the city in 1923, he took with him many memories of the backyard stables, alleys, and fences in that neighborhood—places where he had once played and which he used as the settings for Penrod's many adventures.

Clumsy at sports and disliking rough games, Booth was always a book-loving boy. As a small child, he would interrupt his play to listen to his parents read to him. As a schoolboy, he eagerly tackled the works of Shakespeare, novels by European writers such as Victor Hugo and Charles Dickens, and histories of the United States and England. Not everything he read was so substantial, however. He loved the ten-cent "thrillers" that were enormously popular in the late 1800s—short, action-filled books featuring villains and heroes with colorful names such as Deadwood Dick. Years later, Tarkington recalled his fascination with those "dime novel" characters and wove them into the Penrod stories. In the first *Penrod* book, readers meet the young scamp sneaking off to his sawdust-box hideaway in the stable to compose his own gory tale of blood titled

HARoLD RAMoREZ THE RoADAGENT
OR WiLD LiFE AMoNG THE
ROCKY MTS.

As much as young Booth liked to read, he also liked to write. Before he was school-age, he dictated tales about California gold fields to his indulgent sister Haute, older by eleven years. Later, he filled copybooks and journals with his "literary" scribblings. By the time he was thirteen, he was even writing plays. His first dramatic effort, staged in the stable hayloft behind his house, was a fourteen-act melodrama about the famous outlaw Jesse James. Though the audience of squirming neighborhood children was only mildly impressed, Booth was inspired enough to keep writing plays for the next fifty years.

Booth's other passion as a child was drawing. He wanted to become an illustrator when he grew up, and among those who encouraged him was the Hoosier poet James Whitcomb Riley. Riley first became acquainted with the Tarkingtons in the 1870s while working for the *Indianapolis Journal*. He spent many afternoons and evenings at their house, at first to court Haute and later to enjoy the family's company. Like Booth, Riley was fond of drawing, and in time the two developed a warm relationship. One day in 1886, when Booth was still a teenager, Riley sought the boy's advice for the cover design of new book on which he was working. Booth examined the drawing, then added strokes of his own. A satisfied Riley had *The Boss Girl* published with Booth's contribution and called the young artist his "collaborator."

"No other boy," Booth would later write, "could ever have had precisely just such a friend."

Despite being well-bred and well-read, Booth was not a model pupil. He attended carefully to his schoolwork his first three years, but in the fourth grade he rebelled when his teacher took a dislike to him. After that, the classroom became a sort of prison, and when he was a junior at Shortridge High School he broke out. He played hookey for nine weeks, a period which ended with his withdrawal from school. His parents, though disappointed, were understanding, and they sent him the following fall to Phillips Exeter Academy, a private school in New Hampshire. Two years there helped Booth mature and, in his words, "open my eyes to the world." After that he attended Purdue University in West Lafayette, Indi-

A letter to James Whitcomb Riley, in which Tarkington thanks his old friend for dedicating a poem to him.

ana, for a year and then transferred to Princeton University, an old and prestigious school in New Jersey rich with colonial history.

Booth agreed to the transfer as a favor to his mother; she had long dreamed of her son attending an Eastern college. He never regretted the move, however, and soon was busy writing and drawing sketches for literary magazines, editing the yearbook, singing bass solos for the glee club, and playing the lead role in a musical comedy he helped write. His easygoing personality and quick wit attracted him to classmates, and his dormitory room was often crowded late into the night with joke-telling, banjo-playing, cigarette-smoking friends. He once humorously noted that he got an education at Princeton, "though it seems to me that I *tried* to avoid *that* as much as possible."

When he finally left Princeton in 1893 (he was ineligible to receive a degree because he did not have the required background in classical languages), he didn't depart empty-handed. He had benefited from exposure to new people and ideas. He had made lasting friendships. And he had perfected the art of having a rollicking good time, the kind he heartily recommended to all who asked.

"Between two and five A.M. every night take unlimited Beer, Bananas, Cheese Sandwiches, Chocolate Creams and Cake, Lemon Ice and a Welsh Rarebit," he advised a classmate a few months after leaving Princeton.

"Don't go to bed too early."

* * *

When Booth Tarkington returned to Indianapolis in 1893, he had no firm plans, other than to try to make a living as a free-lance writer and illustrator. His parents, as usual, were patient and supportive. They welcomed him back, made him comfortable in an upstairs bedroom, and offered words of encouragement as he doggedly set about writing short stories and drawing pen-and-ink sketches. When all he received for his efforts were rejection slips, his parents bore their disappointment quietly. They urged him not to give up.

Neighbors and acquaintances weren't nearly as tolerant, however. In their opinion, Tarkington had become a loafer who slept too long during the day, played too hard at night, and raced too merrily around the city in a red-wheeled runabout. What neighbors didn't know is that, long after everyone else was in bed, Tarkington was usually at his desk writing, sometimes until dawn. He was reluctant to reveal how long he wrote for fear people would think him foolish and unproductive. That concern was confirmed one morning when, after an unusually long writing session, he met the milkman outside his house:

> "You been up all night?" he (the milkman) asked.
> "Yes," I answered.
> "What you been doin'?" he went on.
> "Working," said I.
> "Workin'!" said he. "What at?"
> "Writing," said I.
> "How long?" said he.
> "Since yesterday noon," said I. "About sixteen hours."
> "My God," said he. "You must have lots of time to waste!"

Had it not been for the generosity of his parents—and an inheritance from a rich uncle who was the former governor of California—Tarkington likely would have been forced to end his literary "apprenticeship." Between 1893 and 1898 all he earned from his drawings and stories was a mere $22.50. With money not a concern, however, Tarkington kept returning to his desk, trying to teach himself how to write. "I strained and fought with writing, striving to accomplish styles and to chime style with subject," he later recalled. He also kept turning out the kinds of fiction he thought people wanted: sentimental romances set in foreign lands in distant times.

TARKINGTON, BOOTH

598 N. Penn St.
April 25, 1895

Mrs. May Wright Sewall,
343 N. Penn. St.,
City.

My dear Mrs. Sewall—

I thank you very
much for the honor your
request does me. It puffs
me up exceedingly and adds
to my dignity, so that I re-
gret the more that it will
be impossible for
become a slander
present occasion.
mentable habits
have taken to i
in the night and

An 1895 letter to Indianapolis educator and suffragette May Wright Sewall, in which Tarkington mentions his "lamentable habits" of working late into the night.

> *. . . If I had known [of the occasion] a week or so ago, I should have gone into training and gradually shifted my rest . . .*
> *Very sincerely yours,*
> *Newton Booth Tarkington*

Booth Tarkington, 1899.

Despite his earnest efforts, the rejection slips kept coming—so fast that Tarkington later joked his manuscripts "must have been stopped and returned from Philadelphia; they didn't seem to have had time to get all the way to New York and back."

In April 1898, after five years of having "flooded the mails" with drawings and stories, Tarkington pulled from his desk a manuscript he had begun soon after college. It occurred to him, upon rereading it, to change the opening scenes from Maine to Indiana. And instead of reaching back into history, he decided to set the action in the present—the 1890s. He also decided to model his hero on a Princeton classmate who had recently died and whom he had much admired as a "gentleman." To his new, more realistic work of fiction, he penned the title *The Gentleman from Indiana*.

Within a few months after Tarkington finished that story, his sister Haute visited New York and, without her brother's knowledge, showed another of his manuscripts to the publisher S.S. McClure. Although McClure wasn't interested in *Monsieur Beaucaire*, an eighteenth-century romance, the strong-willed Haute didn't give up easily. She told McClure that her brother was working on a new novel about Indiana. Sensing that a "Hoosier story" might have possibilities, McClure agreed to look at it, and Haute persuaded Tarkington to mail him a copy. Bracing himself for another rejection slip, Tarkington waited one week, then another, for McClure's reply. What he received instead was a letter from Hamlin Garland, one of the finest writers of realistic fiction in America.

"Mr. McClure has given me your manuscript, *The Gentleman from Indiana*, to read. You are a novelist," Garland's letter began.

For Tarkington, who had spent many long, lonely nights practicing his craft, that letter was a gift "that changed everything for me."

* * *

The next decade was a busy, though unsettled, one for the young gentleman-turned-writer from Indiana. He wrote two more best-selling novels. He sold numerous short stories and articles to the nation's leading magazines. He teamed up with another writer to compose more than a half-dozen plays, one of which was a smash hit on Broadway. He even campaigned for and was elected to the Indiana legislature as a Republican. His career in the intensely competitive world of Hoosier politics was short; illness forced him to retire after serving only two years. But the experience inspired him to write stories about political life that were admired by President Theodore Roosevelt and that earned him an invitation to lunch at the White House.

That same decade was also a time of personal turmoil for Tarkington. In June 1902 he married Louisa Fletcher, the daughter of a prominent Indianapolis banker. The marriage was never a happy one, and it ended in divorce in 1911. While still married, the couple spent much time in Europe, with Tarkington often leaving for long stretches to attend to his playwriting in New York. Eventually Tarkington grew weary of traveling back and forth across the Atlantic, and he grew tired of New York as well. With his spirits low, he added to his problems by drinking heavily—too heavily. By early 1912 he realized that he was killing himself with alcohol and that, if he was to have a productive life, he had to quit drinking. On January 16, 1912, he did quit, never to touch alcohol again. Recalling that day, he said, "I suddenly decided I preferred to die sober."

Having made that important decision, he began making others, among them to marry Susanah Robinson of Dayton, Ohio. The two were wed in November 1912, with Susanah joining him in the old homestead in Indianapolis. Feeling settled at last and full of renewed energy, Tarkington then began what became the most creative phase of his career.

WHEN TARKINGTON arrived in New York in January 1899 to meet with S. S. McClure, who had recently agreed to publish *The Gentleman from Indiana*, he was greeted like a celebrity. "You are to be the greatest of the new generation," McClure declared when Tarkington entered his office. Editors and writers then took turns welcoming Tarkington, and when he was introduced later that morning to the distinguished journalist Ida Tarbell, McClure again exclaimed: "This is to be the most famous young man in America."

Though McClure was known for extravagant statements, he had a reputation for spotting talent, and he predicted correctly that this first novel by an unknown writer from the Midwest would be a success. Sales of *The Gentleman from Indiana* were brisk from the start, and twice in 1900 it made the monthly best-seller lists. In the following decades, it was reissued and reprinted numerous times, translated into at least six languages, excerpted in other books, and made into a movie. Though Tarkington himself grew to dislike the novel, *The Gentleman from Indiana* did for him what his earlier manuscripts had not done: it launched his literary career.

The story was about a recent college graduate named John Harkless who leaves the East, buys a rundown newspaper in Plattville, Indiana, and works to improve his community by ridding it of corrupt politicians. In the course of his campaign for justice and decency, Harkless has to contend with a mob of lawless rowdies known as the Whitecaps. In the end he drives out the troublemakers and wins the affection of the beautiful Helen Sherwood.

Loaded with melodrama and sentiment, *The Gentleman from Indiana* fit the literary tastes of the times. Americans in the late 1800s loved "romantic" fiction, and Tarkington's idealized characters possessed everything readers wanted in their heroes and heroines: virtue, intelligence, and charm. The story also possessed an acceptable ending; readers approved of "good guys" overcoming evil.

Though romance dominated the novel and helped make it a hot seller, *The Gentleman from Indiana* had a realistic setting, something not often found in the fiction of that era. Americans in the 1890s were accustomed to books about mythical kingdoms in faraway lands. But only a limited number of novels accurately portrayed life in the United States, especially in regions outside New England. In *The Gentleman from Indiana* Tarkington sought to satisfy readers' curiosity about the Midwest by describing the customs, dress, and language of late nineteenth-century Hoosiers. He also sought to defend his native state. During his student days at Exeter and Princeton, he discovered that his Eastern classmates viewed Midwesterners as inferior and that they ignored Tarkington's Hoosier origin "with conscious tact . . . It was as if I had a physical defect." Proud of Indiana and its people, Tarkington used his novel to show that Midwestern life was every bit as pleasant, if not more so, than life in the East. And he reminded Eastern readers that the land west of the Alleghenies was populated with "dear, good people."

Though it can still be found in libraries, *The Gentleman from Indiana* isn't read much anymore. That's partly because the language, by today's standards, seems too flowery and old-fashioned. But just as Edward Eggleston's *The Hoosier School-Master* remains valuable for its recording of backwoods Indiana life in the 1850s and just as James Whitcomb Riley's poems are valued for their portrayal of Hoosier farm and village life a decade later, Tarkington's novel remains useful as a social history of the state in the late 1800s.

"Just as Eggleston and Riley left records of their respective generations," the Hoosier writer Meredith Nicholson commented in 1921, "so Mr. Tarkington . . . depicts his own day with the effect of contributing a third panel in a series of historical paintings."

Between 1912 and 1924 he composed several successful plays, including the enormously popular *Clarence*. He wrote several critically acclaimed novels, including the two that earned him Pulitzer Prizes.

He also began to produce his humorous tales about young people, especially boys. Among the memorable characters he created were Hedrick Madison, the pushy younger brother in *The Flirt*, and William Sylvanus Baxter, the hopelessly-in-love adolescent in *Seventeen*. From his imagination, too, came that mischievous twelve-year-old named Penrod Schofield, who instantly won the hearts of Americans everywhere and whose adventures soon became a treasured part of the nation's literature.

* * *

Penrod was created during the early months of 1913. Susanah Tarkington had been reading a novel about young schoolboys in England and, upon finishing it, gave the book to her husband. Unlike Susanah, however, Tarkington wasn't impressed with what he read, insisting that "no boy ever talked like the puppets in that story." Then why not write about boys as they really were? asked Susanah. Perhaps he would, Tarkington replied. Several weeks later he called Susanah to his study and read her "Penrod and the Pageant," a comic tale inspired by an experience in his own youth, in which he was forced to wear an outrageously silly costume in a charity play. That Penrod story led to others, and before long magazines were outbidding each other to publish the tales. When the book *Penrod* appeared the following year, sales were so strong that Tarkington eventually wrote two more volumes—*Penrod and Sam* in 1916 and *Penrod Jashber* in 1929. By the time Tarkington died in 1946, total sales of the *Penrod* books exceeded a million copies.

The sentiment and melodrama that had marked Tarkington's earlier work were nowhere to be found in these stories.

By then, Tarkington was convinced that readers were better served by literature that emphasized "realism" over "romance," and like a growing number of American writers, he increasingly tried to inject truth into his fiction. In the Penrod stories he worked especially hard to make Penrod and his pals appear as real people. As Tarkington once noted: "Penrod has been a success because it has kept to *true* boy and avoided book-and-stage boy."

To make Penrod seem believable, Tarkington wrote about common, everyday incidents in a boy's life. Unlike young Jim Hawkins in *Treasure Island*, Penrod doesn't sail the high seas and return home with gold. Unlike Peter in *Peter Pan*, he doesn't fly to Never-Never Land and battle evil pirates. And unlike Tom Sawyer and Huckleberry Finn in Mark Twain's classic novels, he doesn't witness a murder, attend his own funeral, or float down the Mississippi River on a raft.

What Penrod does do, while growing up in a pleasant neighborhood in a Midwestern city, is to try to avoid boredom. And like all children, he tries to avoid run-ins with adults, though conflicts, of course, are inevitable. Neighborhood pals, such as Sam Williams and the brothers Herman and Verman, help make Penrod's days more interesting. And every now and then, Penrod discovers that life can be deliciously fun—especially when he flings tar at the perfectly well-behaved Georgie Bassett, lures Maurice Levy into drinking his homemade "smallpox medicine," and packs coin-paying youngsters into the stable hayloft to learn about Roderick Magsworth Bitts Jr.'s "famos" aunt.

To find "real-boy" models for Penrod, Tarkington had only to look around his neighborhood. His sister Haute's sons, John and Donald Jameson, grew up across the street from him in Indianapolis, and early in his writing career Tarkington would watch their play almost daily. In addition, when he began to write the Penrod stories, he was able to closely observe Haute's youngest son, Booth Jameson, who at the time was just Penrod's age. Tarkington later noted that Booth

Jameson probably was the main model for Penrod, but he added: "A number of boys in that neighborhood who played in our back yard, unconsciously were writing themselves into that book." Tarkington's vivid memories of his own boyhood experiences also proved valuable in his development of Penrod's personality. "I know what makes Penrod," he commented on another occasion, "because I've been years on the job."

Like other classic books featuring youthful characters, *Penrod* had two audiences. Children found the escapades of the mischievous and irreverent youngster to be quite funny, even hilarious. Few could resist laughing when Penrod imitated the tough kid Rupe Collins. Or when he pretended to be the fearless detective George B. Jashber. Or when he lost control of his senses at the circus and stuffed himself with hot winny-wurst, raspberry lemonade, waffles, peanuts, popcorn, watermelon, and sardines—much to the great distress of his stomach.

But adults enjoyed the stories, too, for reasons of their own. They appreciated Tarkington's skillful use of detail when sketching scenes. They admired how he avoided "hand-me-down boy humor" and instead used language that was fresh and witty. And they were impressed with how he awakened certain feelings in them, feelings of what it was once like to be twelve. When Penrod, bored during arithmetic lesson, imagines himself floating out the classroom window and impressing an entire city with his somersaults in the sky, many adults could smile knowingly.

They, too, had once been a daydreamy child who occasionally "drifted away from the painful land of facts, and floated . . . in a new sea of fancy."

* * *

By the early 1920s, Tarkington not only was producing his best work, but he also had become one of the most beloved

Tarkington was extremely fond of his three nephews, and while traveling in Europe in 1903 and 1904, he wrote them numerous letters hoping to share some of the fun he was having abroad. Tarkington, whose first ambition was to be an artist, playfully illustrated his letters, which years later were collected in the book *Your Amiable Uncle*.

and admired writers in America. Literary critics praised him. Universities awarded him honorary degrees. Booksellers saluted his accomplishments by ranking him, in 1921, as the "most significant contemporary" American author. And the public expressed its respect and affection in various popularity polls. In a 1922 survey of readers by *Literary Digest*, Tarkington was voted the "greatest living American author." When *The New York Times* sponsored a contest that same year asking who the ten greatest living Americans were, Tarkington made the list and was the only writer named.

Always a modest man, Tarkington never boasted about these honors. Some of the contests, in fact, impressed him as "silliness." He was extremely pleased, however, when in 1933 his colleagues awarded him the "Gold Medal" of the National Institute of Arts and Letters, an award previously given to only two other novelists. He was also deeply honored when the American Academy of Arts and Letters presented him with a special medal in 1945. In presenting that award, the distinguished writer Sinclair Lewis said: "Mr. Tarkington . . . has been one of the first, and he remains one of the chief, of all the discoverers of America in literature."

With all the fame came great wealth. Along with the income Tarkington earned from his best-selling books, he profited from the many adaptations of his work—for the stage, radio, and cinema. He was also paid handsomely for his many magazine articles, so handsomely at times that even he was amazed. "My prices astonish me," he once wrote to a friend; "they've climbed steadily, by offers, until I'm rather sorry for the magazines that pay 'em. I've really never asked any particular price: the thing has somehow just done itself."

His growing fortune allowed him to enjoy special comforts and pleasures. In 1917, after having spent many summers in Maine, he built a mansion—sometimes referred to as "the house that Penrod built"—in the seaside community of Kennebunkport. He lived there from May to December each year where, when not writing, he cruised in his forty-five-foot speedboat and entertained friends at his waterside clubhouse known as The Floats. In 1923 he bought another home, a large Tudor-style dwelling on a wooded lot on Meridian Street in Indianapolis, three miles north of the family homestead on Pennsylvania Street. He left the old house to escape the noise, grime, and downtown traffic congestion that years earlier had begun to spoil his neighborhood. Into his new home he carried valuable antiques and paintings, part of his growing art collection.

Had Tarkington wanted, he could easily have afforded to devote more time to hobbies and leisure. But he loved to write, and for the next two decades he followed his long-established routine, which included writing for lengthy stretches every day, including Sundays. His books were always marked by graceful writing; they never gave the impression of strain. Yet he was known to labor tirelessly over manuscripts, and he once confessed that writing novels was "a very painful job— much worse than having measles."

Tarkington continued his writing even through two difficult periods in his life. He developed cataracts and was blind for a while in the late 1920s and early 1930s. Instead of allowing himself to sink into despair, he learned to dictate his stories, and his work went on uninterrupted. Eventually, after undergoing several operations, he regained partial eyesight, though he had to continue to rely on dictation. Earlier, during another time of personal crisis, his writing served as much-needed therapy. When his only child Laurel died in 1923 at a young age, he was left grief-stricken. "I must work: I must go on with this novel. If I shouldn't, I'd be wrecked, I think," he wrote in the spring of that year. Several weeks later he reported, "This work has just about saved me from shipwreck. It's been hard to do it, but it would have been so much harder not to."

As productive as Tarkington was in his later years, he failed to impress literary critics as he once had. By the 1930s a new generation was writing about sex, violence, the meaninglessness of life, and other subjects that Tarkington considered to be in bad taste. Tarkington by then thought of himself as a literary "realist," but he permitted himself to go only so far in realistically describing life. As a result, critics dismissed his work as being too polite and uncomplicated.

Readers ignored the critics, however. Even into the 1940s, they welcomed everything Tarkington wrote and gladly bought his books. During the first half of this century, more than five million copies of his works were sold—and that was in an era before mass-produced, inexpensive paperbacks. The literary critic Carl Van Doren, taking note of the enormous goodwill Americans felt towards Tarkington, wrote in 1939: "No other native novelist besides Mark Twain has been generally popular for so long as the forty years between Tarkington's first novel and his latest."

In the spring of 1946, while working on yet another novel, Tarkington became ill. Two months later, on May 19, he died at his home at age seventy-six. To the vast majority of Americans he was remembered as a master craftsman of humorous stories, as a perceptive observer of his time, and as the beloved creator of Penrod. To his friends he was remembered for his charm, kindness, integrity, and optimism. To Hoosiers, he was remembered as one of the best authors—if not the greatest—that the state had ever produced.

In the years since Tarkington's death, critics have struggled to decide what his place in literary history should be. As one writer observed in the 1940s, "Future historians will not set him among the titans, but they will not ignore him." That assessment has largely proven correct. Tarkington's books don't rank alongside the best in American literature, but the best of his work still deserves to be read. As Tarkington's biographer James Woodress noted in 1954, the gentleman from Indiana possessed a talent that was "large, well disciplined, authentically American."

That talent, Woodress added, is "worth a secure place in twentieth-century literary history."

SUGGESTIONS FOR FURTHER READING

Fennimore, Keith J. *Booth Tarkington*. New York: Twayne Publishers, Inc., 1974.

Holliday, Robert C. *Booth Tarkington*. New York: Doubleday, Page & Company, 1918.

Mayberry, Susanah. *My Amiable Uncle: Recollections about Booth Tarkington*. West Lafayette: Purdue University Press, 1983.

Woodress, James. *Booth Tarkington: Gentleman from Indiana*. Philadelphia: Lippincott, 1954.

PENROD

(FROM CHAPTERS XIII AND XIV)

IT WAS THE HABIT of Penrod's mother not to throw away anything whatsoever until years of storage conclusively proved there would never be a use for it; but a recent house-cleaning had ejected upon the back porch a great quantity of bottles and other paraphernalia of medicine, left over from illnesses in the family during a period of several years. This debris Della, the cook, had collected in a large market basket, adding to it some bottles of flavouring extracts that had proved unpopular in the household; also, old catsup bottles; a jar or two of preserves gone bad; various rejected dental liquids—and other things. And she carried the basket out to the storeroom in the stable.

Penrod was at first unaware of what lay before him. Chin on palms, he sat upon the iron rim of a former aquarium and stared morbidly through the open door at the checkered departing back of Della. It was another who saw treasure in the basket she had left.

Mr. Samuel Williams, aged eleven, and congenial to Penrod in years, sex, and disposition, appeared in the doorway, shaking into foam a black liquid within a pint bottle, stoppered by a thumb.

"Yay, Penrod!" the visitor gave greeting.

"Yay," said Penrod with slight enthusiasm. "What you got?"

"Lickrish water."

"Drinkin's!" demanded Penrod promptly. This is equivalent to the cry of "Biters" when an apple is shown, and establishes unquestionable title.

"Down to there!" stipulated Sam, removing his thumb to affix it firmly as a mark upon the side of the bottle—a check upon gormandizing that remained carefully in place while Penrod drank. This rite concluded, the visitor's eye fell upon the basket deposited by Della. He emitted tokens of pleasure.

"Looky! Looky! Looky there! That ain't any good pile o' stuff—oh, no!"

"What for?"

"Drug store!" shouted Sam. "We'll be partners —"

"Or else," Penrod suggested, "I'll run the drugstore and you be a customer —"

"No! Partners!" insisted Sam with such conviction that his host yielded; and within ten minutes the drug store was doing a heavy business with imaginary patrons. Improvising counters with boards and boxes, and setting forth a very druggish-looking stock from the basket, each of the partners found occupation to his taste—Penrod as salesman and Sam as prescription clerk.

"Here you are, madam!" said Penrod briskly, offering a vial of Sam's mixing to an invisible matron. "This will cure your husband in a few minutes. Here's the camphor, mister. Call again! Fifty cents' worth of pills? Yes, madam. There you are! Hurry up with that dose for the nigger lady, Bill!"

"I'll 'tend to it soon's I get time, Jim," replied the prescription clerk. "I'm busy fixin' the smallpox medicine for the sick policeman downtown."

Penrod stopped sales to watch this operation. Sam had found an empty pint bottle and, with the pursed lips and measuring eye of a great chemist, was engaged in filling it from other bottles. First, he poured into it some of the syrup from the condemned preserves; and a quantity of extinct hair

152

Penrod stopped sales to watch this operation.

Illustration by Gordon Grant, from the 1914 edition of *Penrod*

oil; next the remaining contents of a dozen small vials crypti-
cally labelled with physicians' prescriptions; then some rem-
nants of catsup and essence of beef and what was left in several
bottles of mouthwash; after that a quantity of rejected
flavouring extract—topping off by shaking into the mouth of
the bottle various powders from small pink papers, relics of
Mr. Schofield's influenza of the preceding winter.

Sam examined the combination with concern, appearing
unsatisfied. "We got to make that smallpox medicine good and
strong!" he remarked; and, his artistic sense growing more
powerful than his appetite, he poured about a quarter of the
licorice water into the smallpox medicine.

"What you doin'?" protested Penrod. "What you want to
waste that lickrish water for? We ought to keep it to drink
when we're tired."

"I guess I got a right to use my own lickrish water any way
I want to," replied the prescription clerk. "I tell you, you can't
get smallpox medicine too strong. Look at her now!" He held
the bottle up admiringly. "She's as black as lickrish. I bet you
she's strong all right!"

"I wonder how she tastes?" said Penrod thoughtfully.

"Don't smell so awful much," observed Sam, sniffing the
bottle—"a good deal, though!"

"I wonder if it'd make us sick to drink it?" said Penrod.

Sam looked at the bottle thoughtfully; then his eye, wan-
dering, fell upon Duke, placidly curled up near the door, and
lighted with the advent of an idea new to him, but old, old in
the world—older than Egypt!

"Let's give Duke some!" he cried.

That was the spark. They acted immediately; and a minute
later Duke, released from custody with a competent potion of
the smallpox medicine inside him, settled conclusively their
doubts concerning its effect. The patient animal, accustomed
to expect the worst at all times, walked out of the door, shaking
his head with an air of considerable annoyance, opening and
closing his mouth with singular energy—and so repeatedly
that they began to count the number of times he did it. Sam

thought it was thirty-nine times, but Penrod had counted forty-one before other and more striking symptoms appeared.

All things come from Mother Earth and must return—Duke restored much at this time. Afterward, he ate heartily of grass; and then, over his shoulder, he bent upon his master one inscrutable look and departed feebly to the front yard. . . .

Sam turned to go, but paused. A new straw hat was peregrinating along the fence near the two boys. This hat belonged to someone passing upon the sidewalk of the cross-street; and the someone was Maurice Levy. Even as they stared, he halted and regarded them over the fence with two small, dark eyes. . . .

"Lo, Sam!" said Maurice cautiously. "What you doin'?"

Penrod at that instant had a singular experience—an intellectual shock like a flash of fire in the brain. Sitting in darkness, a great light flooded him with wild brilliance. He gasped!

"What you doin'?" repeated Mr. Levy.

Penrod sprang to his feet, seized the licorice bottle, shook it with stoppering thumb, and took a long drink with histrionic unction.

"What you doin'?" asked Maurice for the third time, Sam Williams not having decided upon a reply.

It was Penrod who answered.

"Drinkin' lickrish water," he said simply, and wiped his mouth with such delicious enjoyment that Sam's jaded thirst was instantly stimulated. He took the bottle eagerly from Penrod.

"A-a-h!" exclaimed Penrod, smacking his lips. "That was a good un!"

The eyes above the fence glistened.

"Ask him if he don't want some," Penrod whispered urgently. "Quit drinkin' it! It's no good any more. Ask him!"

"What for?" demanded the practical Sam.

"Go on and ask him!" whispered Penrod fiercely.

"Say, M'rice!" Sam called, waving the bottle. "Want some?"

"Bring it here!" Mr. Levy requested.

"Come on over and get some," returned Sam, being prompted.

"I can't. Penrod Schofield's after me."

"No, I'm not," said Penrod reassuringly. "I won't touch you, M'rice. I made up with you yesterday afternoon—don't you remember? You're all right with me, M'rice."

Maurice looked undecided. But Penrod had the delectable bottle again, and tilting it above his lips, affected to let the cool liquid purl enrichingly into him, while with his right hand he stroked his middle facade ineffably. Maurice's mouth watered.

"Here!" cried Sam, stirred again by the superb manifestations of his friend. "Gimme that!"

Penrod brought the bottle down, surprisingly full after so much gusto, but withheld it from Sam; and the two scuffled for its possession. Nothing in the world could have so worked upon the desire of the yearning observer beyond the fence.

"Honest, Penrod—you ain't goin' to touch me if I come in your yard?" he called. "Honest?"

"Cross my heart!" answered Penrod, holding the bottle away from Sam. "And we'll let you drink all you want."

Maurice hastily climbed the fence, and while he was thus occupied Mr. Samuel Williams received a great enlightenment. With startling rapidity Penrod, standing just outside the storeroom door, extended his arm within the room, deposited the licorice water upon the counter of the drug store, seized in its stead the bottle of smallpox medicine, and extended it cordially toward the advancing Maurice.

Genius is like that—great, simple, broad strokes!

Dazzled, Mr. Samuel Williams leaned against the wall. He had the sensations of one who comes suddenly into the presence of a chef-d'oeuvre. Perhaps his first coherent thought was that almost universal one on such huge occasions: "Why couldn't *I* have done that!". . .

"You can have all you can drink at one pull, M'rice," said Penrod kindly.

"You said I could have all I want!" protested Maurice, reaching for the bottle.

"No, I didn't," returned Penrod quickly, holding it away from the eager hand.

"He did, too! Didn't he, Sam?"

Sam could not reply; his eyes, fixed upon the bottle, protruded strangely.

"You heard him—didn't you, Sam?"

"Well, if I did say it I didn't mean it!" said Penrod hastily, quoting from one of the authorities. "Looky here, M'rice," he continued, assuming a more placative and reasoning tone, "that wouldn't be fair to us. I guess we want some of our own lickrish water, don't we? The bottle ain't much over two-thirds full anyway. What I meant was, you can have all you can drink at one pull."

"How do you mean?"

"Why, this way: you can gulp all you want, so long as you keep swallering; but you can't take the bottle out of your mouth and commence again. Soon's you quit swallering it's Sam's turn."

"No; you can have next, Penrod," said Sam.

"Well, anyway, I mean M'rice has to give the bottle up the minute he stops swallering."

Craft appeared upon the face of Maurice, like a poster pasted on a wall.

"I can drink so long I don't stop swallering?"

"Yes; that's it."

"All right!" he cried. "Gimme the bottle!"

And Penrod placed it in his hand.

"You promise to let me drink until I quit swallering?" Maurice insisted.

"Yes!" said both boys together.

With that, Maurice placed the bottle to his lips and began to drink. Penrod and Sam leaned forward in breathless excitement. They had feared Maurice might smell the contents of the bottle; but that danger was past—this was the crucial moment. Their fondest hope was that he would make his first swallow a voracious one—it was impossible to imagine a second. They expected one big, gulping swallow and then an explosion, with fountain effects.

Little they knew the mettle of their man! Maurice swallowed once; he swallowed twice—and thrice—and he continued to swallow! No Adam's apple was sculptured on that juvenile throat, but the internal progress of the liquid was not a whit the less visible. His eyes gleamed with cunning and malicious triumph, sidewise, at the stunned conspirators; he was fulfilling the conditions of the draught, not once breaking the thread of that marvellous swallering.

His audience stood petrified. Already Maurice had swallowed more than they had given Duke—and still the liquor receded in the uplifted bottle! And now the clear glass gleamed above the dark contents full half the vessel's length—and Maurice went on drinking! Slowly the clear glass increased in its dimensions—slowly the dark diminished.

Sam Williams made a horrified movement to check him—but Maurice protested passionately with his disengaged arm, and made vehement vocal noises remindful of the contract; whereupon Sam desisted and watched the continuing performance in a state of grisly fascination.

Maurice drank it all! He drained the last drop and threw the bottle in the air, uttering loud ejaculations of triumph and satisfaction.

"Hah!" he cried, blowing out his cheeks, inflating his chest, squaring his shoulders, patting his stomach, and wiping his mouth contentedly. "Hah! Aha! Waha! Wafwah! But that was good!"

The two boys stood looking at him in stupor.

"Well, I gotta say this," said Maurice graciously: "You stuck to your bargain all right and treated me fair."

Stricken with a sudden horrible suspicion, Penrod entered the storeroom in one stride and lifted the bottle of licorice water to his nose—then to his lips. It was weak, but good; he had made no mistake. And Maurice had really drained—to the dregs—the bottle of old hair tonics, dead catsups, syrups of undesirable preserves, condemned extracts of vanilla and lemon, decayed chocolate, ex-essence of beef, mixed dental preparations, aromatic spirits of ammonia, spirits of nitre, alcohol, arnica, quinine, ipecac, sal volatile, nux vomica and licorice water—with traces of arsenic, belladonna and strychnine.

Penrod put the licorice water out of sight and turned to face the others. Maurice was seating himself on a box just outside the door and had taken a package of cigarettes from his pocket.

"Nobody can see me from here, can they?" he said, striking a match. "You fellers smoke?"

"No," said Sam, staring at him haggardly.

"No," said Penrod in a whisper.

Maurice lit his cigarette and puffed showily.

"Well, sir," he remarked, "you fellers are certainly square— I gotta say that much. Honest, Penrod, I thought you was after me! I did think so," he added sunnily; "but now I guess you like me, or else you wouldn't of stuck to it about lettin' me drink it all if I kept on swallering."

He chatted on with complete geniality, smoking his cigarette in content. And as he ran from one topic to another his hearers stared at him in a kind of torpor. Never once did they exchange a glance with each other; their eyes were frozen to Maurice. The cheerful conversationalist made it evident that he was not without gratitude.

"Well," he said as he finished his cigarette and rose to go, "you fellers have treated me nice—and some day you come over to my yard; I'd like to run with you fellers. You're the kind of fellers I like."

Penrod's jaw fell; Sam's mouth had been open all the time. Neither spoke.

"I gotta go," observed Maurice, consulting a handsome watch. "Gotta get dressed for the cotillion right after lunch. Come on, Sam. Don't you have to go, too?"

Sam nodded dazedly.

"Well, good-bye, Penrod," said Maurice cordially. "I'm glad you like me all right. Come on, Sam."

Penrod leaned against the doorpost and with fixed and glazing eyes watched the departure of his two visitors. Maurice was talking volubly, with much gesticulation, as they went; but Sam walked mechanically and in silence, staring at his brisk companion and keeping at a little distance from him.

They passed from sight, Maurice still conversing gayly— and Penrod slowly betook himself into the house, his head bowed upon his chest.

THOUGH TARKINGTON was at the forefront of American writers who created "real boy" characters, he wasn't the first. Tarkington himself credited the famous writer and humorist Mark Twain as being the pioneer. In the mid-1870s, Twain wrote *The Adventures of Tom Sawyer*, a novel featuring Tom Sawyer and Huckleberry Finn, two characters whom readers immediately recognized as typical boys. Prior to that novel, according to Tarkington, "nearly all the boys of fiction were adults with a lisp, or saintly infants, or mischievous eccentrics or merely the sturdy 'young gentlemen' . . . in the English novels."

As much as Tarkington admired Twain's work, he didn't copy it. Tarkington believed that Tom Sawyer and Huck Finn were realistic "only in character"—that is, only in the way they spoke and thought. Referring to Tom and Huck's unusual and exciting adventures, Tarkington wrote, "He [Twain] gave 'em what boys don't get when it came to 'plot.' All that the boy [Mark Twain] had wished to happen, he made happen." Penrod's adventures, in contrast, were much more ordinary. As Tarkington would later write, when explaining the success of Penrod: "The detail—*not plot*—is what has made it."

While details added spice to the Penrod stories, Tarkington avoided writing too precisely about certain subjects. Readers soon discovered that he never depicted boys cursing, being curious about sex, or behaving in a vulgar way. Such omissions bothered literary critics; they said Tarkington couldn't portray children realistically if he avoided mentioning their use of foul language or their sexual interests. But Tarkington argued that some details should be left to the imagination and that not everything had to be depicted to convey "real life."

As innocent as the Penrod stories seem by today's standards, modern readers are likely to be jarred by language of another type: Tarkington's references to African Americans. Black people are casually referred to in his stories as "nigger" and "darky." They are also described in demeaning ways, as when Tarkington writes that the black brothers Herman and Verman are "beings in one of those lower stages of evolution."

What are today's readers to make of such passages? Tarkington, like most writers, was influenced by the attitudes and values of people around him. The painful passages in his work reflect, as writer Scott Sanders noted in 1985, "the prejudices of the author's own time and place and social background." Modern readers should not try to make excuses for the offensive passages or pretend they don't exist. Rather, they should, in the words of Sanders, "see them as an expression of a widely shared racism that we have begun, haltingly and imperfectly, to outgrow."

Illustration by Worth Brehm, from the 1916 edition of *Penrod and Sam*

Penrod, Sam, and the brothers Herman and Verman.

ALONG WITH WRITING humor-filled stories about childhood and adolescence, Tarkington is remembered today for a group of other, much more serious novels. Often referred to as his "midland city" novels, these books documented economic and social change in the American Midwest from the end of the Civil War until after World War I.

Indianapolis served as the model for the fictional midland city of the novels. Tarkington had always felt a special connection to his hometown. "Indianapolis," he once explained, "is sort of a *person*—my uncle or somebody." By choosing a setting he was familiar with, he also could more accurately sketch "real life" in America's heartland. What Tarkington had to say about Indianapolis at the turn of the century could also have been said about St. Louis, Chicago, Columbus, and Kansas City. His novels offered readers insight into the growing pains many Midwestern cities experienced at that time—pains brought on by the growth of industry and big business.

Tarkington began writing the first of his ambitious urban growth narratives in 1914, on the eve of World War I. He had recently remarried and settled in Indianapolis after spending eight years living in Europe and New York. He was surprised, upon his return, to see how much his native town had changed. His astonishment grew when he considered the vast differences between the "modern" Indianapolis and the community of his youth. No longer was the Hoosier capital an oversized country town where like-minded families shared common manners, interests, and backgrounds. It had become a thriving, heavily industrialized city with a diverse population. The pace of life had grown faster, and the air had grown dirtier, much dirtier as coal-fed factories belched out thick clouds of smoke. Everywhere Tarkington looked, starting with his own neighborhood, he saw dirt, grime, and soot.

In *The Turmoil*, the first novel in his "midland city" series, Tarkington examined the conflicts within a family that grew wealthy through business dealings in the early years of the twentieth century. That family represented a new class of rich people in America, those who acquired wealth not through inheritance but through hard work, shrewdness, and a willingness to experiment. In *The Magnificent Ambersons*, published in 1918, Tarkington recorded the decline of an old, socially prominent family in the last decades of the 1800s. At the end of that novel, the Amberson family was shoved aside by the "new rich"—the developers, financiers, and manufacturers who showed imagination in a changing era and who aggressively pursued money, often at any cost.

In 1924 Tarkington completed his series with *The Midlander*. Picking up where *The Turmoil* left off, it told the story of a real-estate developer who dreamed of making his midland city more beautiful and prosperous but who in the end died lonely and unhappy, a victim of the new "industrial America." A few years earlier, in 1921, Tarkington set his novel *Alice Adams* in the same midland city. That story, which many critics consider Tarkington's best work, recorded how the desire for money and social status destroyed a struggling lower-middle-class family. Alice, the charming but vain heroine, reluctantly realized at the novel's end that she must settle for a life as a typist and secretary—and not as a wife in the privileged class.

In all these novels Tarkington's point was not to condemn or applaud the social, economic, or political forces that were changing America. Rather, his purpose was to record dispassionately what he saw around him and to portray his characters as real people living complicated, yet ordinary, lives. For his efforts he was twice awarded the Pulitzer Prize in fiction—for *The Magnificent Ambersons* and for *Alice Adams*. Yet all of his "midland city" stories were well-written, and taken together they provide modern readers with an immensely useful record of a bygone era. As the respected educator and historian Henry Steele Commager noted years ago: "If you want to know what houses looked like, outside and inside; how men and women dressed; how they spoke; how they behaved; you can go to Tarkington. He had an eye for detail."

164

Photos courtesy Susanah Mayberry

(Right) "Papa" John Tarkington.

Below: (left) Susanah Tark-ington. (right) Tarkington's sister, Haute.

(Left) The old homestead at 1100 North Pennsylvania Street in Indianapolis, where Tarkington grew up.

(Below) The dining room of Tarkington's North Meridian Street home, where he moved in 1923 after grime and noise drove him from the old homestead.

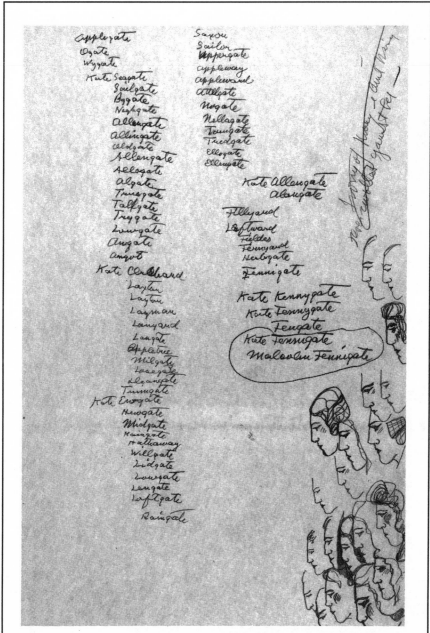

Original manuscript page of *Kate Fennigate* (1943), showing how Tarkington worked to settle on a name for the lead character.

Tarkington at his "Seawood" home in Maine, around 1941, dictating to his secretary Betty Trotter.

Tarkington at his clubhouse "The Floats" with his long-time companion Figaro, around 1944.

Theodore Dreiser

5

THEODORE DREISER

When Caroline Meeber boarded the afternoon train for Chicago her total outfit consisted of a small trunk, which was checked in the baggage car, a cheap imitation alligator skin satchel holding some minor details of the toilet, a small lunch in a paper box and a yellow leather snap purse, containing her ticket, a scrap of paper with her sister's address in Van Buren Street, and four dollars in money. It was in August, 1889. She was eighteen years of age, bright, timid and full of the illusions of ignorance and youth.

S O BEGINS *SISTER CARRIE*, the controversial first novel of Theodore Dreiser, a writer who made a career out of telling the truth as he saw it. Today, nearly a century after it was written, *Sister Carrie* is recognized as a classic in modern American literature. Today, too, Dreiser is celebrated as one of America's most important writers of fiction. But during Dreiser's lifetime and in the years following his death in 1945, the public was slow to appreciate his work. And in Indiana Dreiser was regarded as the "bad boy" among Hoosier authors, the native son whom the home folk preferred not to claim as their own.

That the public failed at first to recognize Dreiser's genius isn't surprising. He didn't write the kind of books early twentieth-century Americans were accustomed to or that they wanted. He composed no tender love stories. He penned no heart-pounding adventure tales set in exotic lands. He sketched no light comedies with clever and cheery endings. Instead, Dreiser wrote fiction that was raw and pessimistic. And he portrayed life in ways that Americans preferred it not be sketched: unpredictable, hopeless, tragic.

Dreiser could write as he did because he knew firsthand about life's harsh side. He grew up in a large, poor, troubled family, never knowing the comforts and security that middle-class writers such as Booth Tarkington enjoyed in their youth. He also grew up feeling inferior to people who had expensive clothes, polished manners, good looks—and money. When he turned to novel-writing, he drew heavily from past experience to create characters who groped for social "acceptance." He also made money, especially the lack of it, a major theme in his fiction. Throughout Dreiser's long, up-and-down literary career, his novels reflected his contempt for an American society that he believed worshipped material "success." His novels also reflected his frustration with a stiff-necked moral code which he deemed hypocritical and repressive.

To most Americans, especially those in Indiana, Dreiser's unconventional views went beyond being offensive. His ideas were thought to be obscene and dangerous, and for years people who didn't like what he wrote tried to suppress his work. But Dreiser believed passionately in the right of artists to express themselves as they chose, and he adamantly refused to give in to his critics. Eventually, the censors backed down. Eventually, too, the public began to recognize Dreiser for what he was: a profoundly original writer who was far ahead of his time, who infused American fiction with a bold new spirit—and who helped make possible the achievements of later writers ranging from Ernest Hemingway to William Faulkner to John Steinbeck.

"He had an enormous influence on American literature during the first quarter of the century—and for a time he was

American literature, the only writer worth talking about in the same breath with the European masters," the journalist Richard Lingeman wrote in 1990 in his massive biography of Dreiser. "He elevated the creative principle to a godhead and encouraged by word and example truthful expression in others."

Seventy-four years earlier in 1916, the novelist Sherwood Anderson made much the same point: "The feet of Dreiser are making a path for us. They are tramping through the wilderness making a path."

* * *

When Theodore Dreiser was born in the latter part of the nineteenth century, most Americans of wealth, power, and status could trace their forebears to Great Britain. Theodore could not. His father, John Paul Dreiser, had emigrated from Germany in 1844. His mother, Sarah Schanab, was born in America, but her background was Czech.

While ancestry didn't help the social standing of Theodore's family, neither did church affiliation. John Paul was an orthodox Roman Catholic, and he insisted that his children be raised in his faith, even though most Protestant Americans at the time looked down on and were suspicious of Catholics. Knocking the Dreisers even farther down the social scale was their lack of formal education. Sarah could not write until her children taught her. And though her offspring had the benefit of some schooling, they were reared in a home rife with ignorance and superstition.

Theodore was the second youngest of thirteen Dreiser children (the first three died at an early age). Shortly before Theodore's birth in Terre Haute on August 27, 1871, John Paul lost his job as manager of a woolen mill, and after that he was often out of work. Sarah, whom Dreiser described as a "dreamy, poetic, impractical soul," did what she could to keep the family together. To pay the rent, she took in railroad workers and miners as boarders. She also washed clothes for local townsfolk. But money was always scarce, and sometimes the Dreiser children had to search along railroad tracks for chunks of coal spilled from trains just to keep the fire burning in their stove.

"I recall cornmeal mush eaten without milk because we had none," Dreiser wrote years later. "I recall clothes so old and so made over and patched that they were a joke."

To save money, the family at times split up, with John Paul and the older children living in one Indiana community, Sarah and the younger children in another. But whenever the Dreisers were united, home life was rarely happy or peaceful. Frustrated because he couldn't pay his debts, the bitter and gloomy John Paul took out his anger on the children, ranting uncontrollably when they disobeyed. The children, turned off by their father's fanatical devotion to the church, ignored him and did as they pleased. Theodore's older sisters became flirts, his older brother Rome gambled and drank whiskey, and his oldest brother Paul earned a reputation as a troublemaker, even getting arrested once for burglary.

Theodore, a quiet, observant boy, was aware of all the tensions at home. He was aware, too, that respectable citizens gossiped over backyard fences about his family, seen wherever it moved as a hard-pressed, quarrelsome, and disorderly clan. "I became mentally colored or tinged," Dreiser recalled later, "with a sense of poverty and defeat and social ill-being in connection with our family that took me years and years, and then only in part, to overcome."

As accustomed as Theodore was to "privation and misery," the winter of 1882 was especially unbearable for the Dreisers. The rent on the family's small cottage in Sullivan, Indiana, was long overdue. The food pantry was bare. John Paul, who was living at the time in Terre Haute, was out of work and unable to send money. Sarah, tired and sick with worry, was overcome with despair.

And then, in Dreiser's words, "behold, a miracle!"

Theodore's eldest brother Paul, who had left home years earlier, changed his name to Dresser, and begun to achieve fame as a songwriter and minstrel-show entertainer, showed up unannounced at the cottage door. He was dressed in a fur coat and silk hat, carried a gold-headed cane, and had wads of money stuffed in his pockets. Heartbroken when he saw how his family was living, he quickly arranged for Sarah and the younger children to move to Evansville, where he escorted them to a comfortably furnished house. He then visited them regularly, bringing treats, telling funny stories, and amusing everyone with songs on the piano. To Theodore, this handsome, generous brother was "like the sun, or a warm, cheering fire. He beamed upon us all . . ."

Paul's return at such a crucial time left a lasting impression on Dreiser—and not solely because the family had been rescued from poverty. Dreiser would come to see Paul's arrival as "luck." And he would increasingly come to believe that luck, or blind chance, played a decisive role in people's lives. The Dreiser family's good fortune, meanwhile, was short-lived. By the summer of 1884, the fun-loving, free-spending Paul had run out of money and left Evansville to rejoin a touring minstrel show. Sarah and her rootless brood had no choice but to move again.

After spending a few months in Chicago, the family settled in northern Indiana, in the quiet county-seat town of Warsaw. There, for the first time, Theodore began to enjoy school. There, too, he began to read more widely and to receive encouragement from attentive and sympathetic teachers. In many respects, Theodore was happier in Warsaw than he had been any other place. But he continued to be hurt by small-town gossip about his clamorous family. And by 1887 he could tolerate the hurtful wisecracks no more. Dreaming of a better life, he announced that summer that he was leaving home, and, like the fictional Carrie Meeber in his novel, he soon boarded a train for Chicago. Not quite sixteen, he departed with only a bag of clothes, some cold chicken and apples packed in a shoebox, and six dollars borrowed from his mother.

But, as he later wrote: "Neither fear nor loneliness possessed me . . . New land, new life, was what my heart was singing!"

* * *

Chicago in the late 1800s was a boom town. Between 1870 and 1890 nearly a million people poured into the city, most from Midwestern farms and villages. Many of the new arrivals were like Dreiser, sons and daughters of immigrants from Germany, Ireland, Poland, Greece, Scandinavia, and Russia. "Chicago was the stew-pan of creation," wrote the Hoosier humorist and playwright George Ade, who worked as a Chicago newspaperman in the late 1800s. "It was a roaring, brawling multitude of suddenly assembled specimens from all parts of the world."

The newcomers were lured to Chicago by the promise of jobs in newly opened department stores and high-rise office buildings, in factories and foundries, in stockyards and lumberyards and rail yards. They were lured, too, by the prospect of glamorous living. Chicago's lamplit streets were lined with grand hotels, elegant restaurants, glittering shops, and fashionable theaters, in and out of which passed stylishly dressed seekers of fun. To the "hopeful and the hopeless," as Dreiser described the new arrivals, Chicago was more than a hub of power and pleasure; it was an enchanted kingdom on the Illinois prairie.

As his fictional character Carrie had, Dreiser initially found the swirl of activity to be thrilling. "Beautiful!" he wrote years later, recalling his early impressions of Chicago. "Cars, people, lights, shops! The odor and flavor of the city, the vastness of its reaches, seemed to speak or sing or tinkle like a living, breathing thing." But fascinated as Dreiser was, city living worked no quick magic in his life. Just as Carrie had to settle for a low-paying job in a shoe factory, the skinny and weak-muscled Dreiser had to labor at menial jobs as a dishwasher, stove cleaner, and stockboy in a hardware store. He clung to his dream of "becoming a great man" and remained determined to break out of his poverty. But as the months passed, he grew weary of dirty, dead-end jobs. And he grew envious of "great men" in clean suits who were chauffeured from stately mansions to spacious offices to fancy clubs. "How wonderful! Think of the glory of being rich—horses and carriages and servants," he wrote. "Ah—if it could only be so . . ."

In 1889, after nearly two years of eking out a living, a depressed Dreiser needed a guardian angel to rescue him, and, through another stroke of luck, his rescuer came. Miss Mildred Fielding, one of his teachers in Warsaw, appeared one day at the hardware business where he worked and offered to send him to Indiana University in Bloomington. Fielding, who by then was principal at a Chicago high school, had seen potential in the shy, sensitive, shabbily clothed Dreiser and had always wanted to help him. "Read philosophy and history," she urged her former student at their reunion. "You will see how life works and how mistaken or untrue most beliefs are . . . You have the capacity for rising high in the world, and I want you to do it."

Amazed at his good fortune, Dreiser didn't need any prodding. At summer's end, he packed his belongings in a battered trunk, said good-bye to his family who had joined him in Chicago, and hurried back to his native state. He was eighteen, excited, and eager. He was also clueless as to what he would do once he arrived in Bloomington.

* * *

Dreiser earned passing grades as a freshman at Indiana University, but college wasn't for him. He felt uncomfortable around his wealthier, better-looking classmates, made few friends, and was restless. By June 1890 he was back in Chicago, unwilling to return for his sophomore year. The experience had changed him, however. He came home feeling "more courageous, more ambitious," and he was convinced that Miss Fielding was right—he did have the capacity to rise.

How to rise was another matter, however. His eyes, as he later noted, were still "constantly fixed on people in positions far above my own. Those who interested me most were bankers, millionaires, artists, executive leaders, the real rulers of the world." He was fascinated as well by newspaper people whom he imagined led exciting lives, dashing here and there to interview the rich and the famous. In the spring of 1892, after nearly two years of driving a laundry wagon and toiling at odd jobs, Dreiser decided to prove he was "no common man." He began haunting the newsroom at the *Chicago Globe*, then one of the city's poorer papers, hoping to get hired as a reporter. He had never before pursued a goal with unswerving determination, but this time was different. When an editor agreed to give him a tryout if he first peddled some books, Dreiser took to the streets, sold the books, and then began working furiously to show he could gather news. When through sheer luck Dreiser got a big "scoop" that summer, he was hired full-time.

It was during those early newspaper days, Dreiser later recalled, that he increasingly felt the creative urge swelling up within him. "I seethed to express myself," he wrote. Yet, as a result of his limited schooling, Dreiser knew little about writing. His grammar and spelling were bad, his sentences long and clumsy, his prose repetitive. What he did possess, however, were keen powers of observation. And he had a knack for communicating what he saw and heard, often in language that was vivid, powerful, and drenched in details. Through hard work and an overwhelming desire to succeed, he gradually rose in the world of journalism, moving in 1892 to the prestigious *St. Louis Globe-Democrat*, later to the *Pittsburgh Dispatch*, and eventually to New York, where he established himself as a free-lance magazine writer and editor.

Dreiser's move across America in the last decade of the nineteenth century—the Gilded Age—came at a crucial time in his development as a writer. As he roamed the streets of the nation's great cities, he saw factories being built, fortunes being made, and families living lavishly in homes resembling palaces. He saw vast business empires being created by wealthy industrialists and financiers such as Andrew Carnegie, J. P. Morgan, and John D. Rockefeller.

But Dreiser also observed that the growth of industry in America had another, darker side. He saw that the people who labored in the factories, mills, and mines—many of them immigrants—often worked sixty hours a week, earned pitifully low wages, and receive no benefits. He saw that most lived in crowded tenements in grimy neighborhoods that reeked with decaying garbage and which were breeding grounds for disease. He saw that violence and suffering and despair were part of daily life for the less privileged and that, instead of escaping from poverty, too many were crushed by it.

To Dreiser, no stranger to poverty himself, his observations reinforced what he already knew: the gap between rich and poor in America was wide. His observations also gave shape to his personal philosophy. He was increasingly convinced that life was an unrelenting struggle, that what people struggled for was material success, and that most men and women exhausted themselves chasing after "things"—a big house, fashionable clothes, expensive possessions. He was convinced, too, that people who achieved success didn't always do so by their own efforts, but rather due to chance or circumstance. And Dreiser was certain that those who acquired riches were never completely satisfied. In his view society tricked people into thinking money bought happiness, and man—"a poor, blind fool"—was unable to see through the trickery.

In the fall of 1899, Dreiser settled into life in New York with his new bride, Sara White, a schoolteacher from Missouri. But his mind was not settled. He had seen and heard too much in industrialized America, and now he seethed to pour out his discontent and to express himself in a novel. He took out a sheet of yellow paper and randomly wrote the title "Sister Carrie" across the top.

He kept writing.

* * *

When asked years later how his first novel was born, Dreiser said "my mind was a blank except for the name. I had no idea who or what she was to be."

But Dreiser knew during that autumn of 1899 that he wanted to record the experiences of people, rich and poor, living in America's cities. He also wanted to record those experiences as honestly as possible. It always annoyed him when magazine editors insisted that he include "sweetness" in his articles, even if that meant twisting the facts and painting a distorted picture. In *Sister Carrie*, he determined, life would be sketched as he had observed it. "Here is a book that is close to life," he would later say. And in 1902 he would tell a newspaper interviewer: "In *Sister Carrie* all phases of life touched upon are handled truthfully. I have not tried to gloss over any evil any more than I have stopped to dwell upon it."

Dreiser began his "close-to-life" novel by having young Carrie Meeber, an innocent country girl from Wisconsin, move to Chicago where she is ill-prepared and fearful but determined to succeed. Though she quickly discovers that life there will not be easy, she manages to get by for a while. But then she becomes ill and loses her job. Her hopes for a better life fade.

At that point Dreiser could have pleased readers and avoided controversy if he had arranged for Carrie to marry a hard-working, respectable young man with whom she lived happily. Instead, Carrie, who longs for the fancy clothes and finery that other people have, lives with—but never marries—

a smooth-talking traveling salesman who gives her money and makes her comfortable in a cozy apartment. Later, she becomes attracted to a prosperous married man named George Hurstwood and eventually moves with him to New York. Then, just when readers thought Dreiser should have punished Carrie for becoming romantically involved with the two men, she starts succeeding in her career as an actress. The novel closes with Carrie living in a luxurious apartment, earning a huge salary, and enjoying audiences' cheers "ringing in her ears." At no point in the novel is she condemned by Dreiser, a sign to many people of that era that he didn't consider her behavior "immoral."

The sign was intentional; Dreiser didn't consider Carrie to have "sinned." From his perspective, Carrie lived as she did in order to survive in a brutal, unjust world. From Dreiser's perspective, too, Carrie's sexual life wasn't all that different from the sexual lives of other women. He knew how Americans in the late 1800s expected females to behave and how readers expected them to be portrayed in literature: women were to resist the "advances" of men and to be intimate only with their husbands. But Dreiser also knew that in everyday life women and men who weren't marriage partners sometimes had "affairs." Writers who denied such realities were, in Dreiser's words, guilty of "the trashiest lie."

Dreiser neither had to lie nor do much inventing when he devised the central plot for *Sister Carrie*. Carrie's story was based loosely on the life of Dreiser's older sister Emma, who moved to Chicago several years before Dreiser did, lived with an architect, and then became involved with a married man named L. A. Hopkins. In 1886, Emma and Hopkins fled Chicago with thirty-five hundred dollars that Hopkins had stolen from the saloon where he worked. The pair traveled by train to Canada and then to New York City—just as Carrie and George Hurstwood do after Hurstwood steals ten thousand dollars from the Chicago saloon he manages. To avoid arrest and probably to ease his conscience, Hopkins returned

When Theodore Dreiser moved to New York in the mid-1890s, he began seeing more of his brother, Paul Dresser, who by then was a successful songwriter in the city. With Paul's help, Dreiser became the editor of *Ev'ry Month*, a magazine that promoted songs published by a company Paul partly owned. One day in 1897 Paul was at the publishing office, experimenting with new tunes on the piano. He asked his brother to be a good "sport" and give him an idea for a song.

"Me?" Dreiser later recalled himself saying. "I can't write those things. Why don't you write something about a State or a river? Look at 'My Old Kentucky Home,' 'Dixie,' 'Old Black Joe'—why don't you do something like that, something that suggests a part of America? People like that. Take Indiana— what's the matter with it—the Wabash River? It's as good as any other river, and you were 'raised' beside it."

Delighted with the suggestion, Paul insisted that Dreiser write some lyrics. Grudgingly, Dreiser penned the first verse of "On the Banks of the Wabash"—words which Paul set to music. The result was a hit song, soon played and whistled across America. In Indiana, it eventually was awarded the highest of honors: it was chosen as the official state song in 1913.

> *Round my Indiana homestead wave the cornfields,*
> *In the distance loom the woodlands clear and cool.*
> *Often times my thoughts revert to scenes of childhood,*
> *Where I first received my lessons, nature's school.*
>
> *But one thing there is missing in the picture,*
> *Without her face it seems so incomplete.*
> *I long to see my mother in the doorway,*
> *As she stood there years ago, her boy to greet.*

Paul Dresser.

Cover of sheet music for "On the Banks of the Wabash."

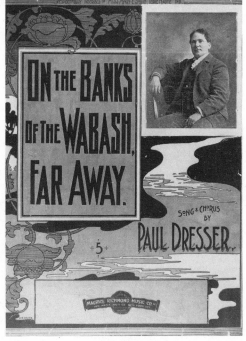

the money. In *Sister Carrie*, Hurstwood returns most of the stolen money after being pursued by detectives. But he keeps some to finance a new life for himself and Carrie, who still craves pleasure and hungers for stylish clothes.

Eventually Emma left Hopkins and settled into the role of a traditional nineteenth-century homemaker in New York. Carrie also leaves Hurstwood, who realizes too late that he has disgraced himself by stealing and leaving his family. But while Hurstwood slides into poverty and becomes a bum who begs in breadlines—thus fulfilling the public's expectation that bad behavior should be punished—Carrie manages through hard work and luck to acquire all the money she needs. Like Hurstwood, however, she isn't happy. And like so many of Dreiser's characters, she fails to understand that what she was chasing—the American dream of success—was a dream that would always leave her unfulfilled.

"All her nature was stirred to unrest now," Dreiser wrote of Carrie at the novel's stark conclusion. "She was already the old, mournful Carrie—the desireful Carrie,—unsatisfied."

* * *

When Dreiser finished writing *Sister Carrie* in the spring of 1900, he assumed that the hard work was behind him and that he needed only to take his manuscript to "a reputable publisher and get it published. Presto—fame and fortune."

He assumed wrong.

Harper and Brothers, then one of the country's leading publishing companies, quickly rejected the manuscript, saying readers would be too offended by the novel's realism, especially by Carrie's "illicit relations" with men. Undeterred, Dreiser next sent the manuscript to Doubleday, Page and Company, where an editor called *Sister Carrie* one of the best novels he had ever read. A contract to publish the book was signed, and an elated Dreiser thought all was well. But Frank Doubleday, the company's senior member, was in Europe at the time, and when he finally read the manuscript he thought the story was so immoral and badly written that he tried to call the deal off. Dreiser refused.

Doubleday eventually published *Sister Carrie* but resisted promoting or advertising it. As a result, only 456 copies sold, earning Dreiser a mere $68.40 in royalties. Moreover, most of the country's major literary magazines didn't review the book, and many of the newspapers that did considered it vulgar, gloomy, and "unhealthful in tone." As one reviewer noted, "the effect is depressing." Declared another: "You would never dream of recommending [it] to another person to read."

Convinced that Doubleday had done everything it could to "kill" his book, a bitter Dreiser resumed work on a second novel, *Jennie Gerhardt*. As in *Sister Carrie*, Dreiser sought to poke through the stereotype of the "sinful" woman and show that other factors—namely, social forces and chance—are usually at work when "good" girls go "bad." As much as Dreiser wanted to finish *Jennie*, however, his despondency made it difficult for him to concentrate. Making matters worse, he was short on money again, and his two-year-old marriage was showing signs of strain. Frustrated, he left New York and traveled south, hoping his travels would cheer him up. But his mood remained dark, and he even feared he was going crazy. In February 1903 he returned to New York, "still in the dumps"—as he wrote an editor—"in regard to *Sister Carrie.*"

He tried to resume writing articles for magazines, but he lacked inspiration. Though desperate for money, he was too proud to ask for help from his wife, Sara, who was back in Missouri. He was also too ashamed to seek handouts from family members and friends. Within a few months he was down to his last dollars and surviving on half a loaf of bread and a bottle of milk a day; to stretch his funds, he resorted to scavenging in a nearby market, picking from the gutter apples or potatoes which occasionally fell from wagons. Back in his dingy room in a cheap boardinghouse in Brooklyn, he tried to sleep but was terrorized by frightful dreams that made him leap from bed. Alone and lonely, he had come to resemble his own fictional creation—the defeated George Hurstwood at the end of *Sister Carrie*.

"What purpose was served by so vast, go grim, so merciless a strife?" Dreiser later wrote of his suffering. "There was none. It was all a great cruel mystery—a vast, shapeless, interminable and horrible unrest and now at last it had me in its clutches, it would not let me go and I was to sink back—sick, weary, dissatisfied—in the gloom and mystery of it."

Though he contemplated suicide during those bleak months, he eventually found himself rescued again by none other than his brother Paul. A successful songwriter living in New York at the time, Paul hadn't seen his younger brother in years when he suddenly encountered him on the street one day. Shocked at how thin and ragged Dreiser looked, Paul insisted on helping and immediately made arrangements to send him to a health camp outside the city. Dreiser protested at first, not wanting to admit need. But Paul convinced him otherwise, and Dreiser was soon getting plenty of rest, proper food, and vigorous exercise at a camp which catered to exhausted businessmen. When he left two months later, he was much improved physically and mentally and grateful that his nervous breakdown had not cost him his life.

He proceeded slowly after that, working for a while as a laborer on the railroad. But eventually he returned to magazine writing and editing, and by 1905 he was the editor of the popular monthly *Smith's* magazine. Within two more years he had a large staff, a handsome salary, and a high-powered job as editor-in-chief of Butterick Publications, where he oversaw three enormously popular magazines that appealed to tradition-minded women. On the surface all seemed well in Dreiser's life. He was living comfortably, savoring his lofty position, and enjoying the opportunity to associate with other writers, especially a cocky young Baltimore newspaperman named H. L. Mencken.

But the novelist within him was restless. And in his four-year journey from a flophouse to a luxurious and lordly office, he had never stopped thinking about *Sister Carrie*.

*   *   *

In 1900, as Dreiser had painfully learned, the country wasn't ready for a novel as honest and as sexually explicit as *Sister Carrie* was. But times were changing. And in early 1907 Dreiser, who had repeatedly looked for ways to get *Sister Carrie* before the public, found what he had been seeking—a publisher who would reissue the novel and who would be courageous enough to promote it.

The new publisher was Ben Dodge, who with some of Dreiser's money introduced *Sister Carrie* anew to readers on May 18, 1907, just weeks before Dreiser assumed his new duties at Butterick. Unlike its introduction in 1900, the reborn *Sister Carrie* sold briskly, and within the first three months sales exceeded forty-six hundred copies. Equally pleasing to Dreiser was that literary critics, who had been unaware of or indifferent to *Sister Carrie* seven years earlier, now took notice of the novel and wrote favorable reviews. Some still called the book "harmful" and warned that it should be "shunned." But others proclaimed it "a work of genius" and "literature of high class."

"One of the most important books of the year," declared a critic for the *Washington Evening Star*. Another reviewer, writing in a New Orleans newspaper, pronounced *Sister Carrie* the "strongest piece of realism we have yet met with in American fiction."

The critics were complimentary in 1907 partly because American literary criticism had matured. Reviewers realized that even though Dreiser was a bad stylist—a writer whose prose was ponderous and ungrammatical—that didn't mean *Sister Carrie* was a clumsily constructed story. On the contrary, the reviewers who read *Sister Carrie* with fresh eyes in 1907 realized Dreiser had crafted an extraordinarily powerful tale. They admired him especially for examining a wide range of human life, for recording that which was unpleasant and ugly, and for forcing Americans to confront issues—namely sex—which had previously been glossed over in literature.

Ordinary Americans were slower to share the critics' enthusiasm. As the writer Alfred Kazin noted in recent times, to have been an early admirer of *Sister Carrie* "was just as dangerous as trying to shoot the President." Still, reluctant readers continued to buy the controversial book, which eventually was translated into more than twenty languages and since then has remained continuously in print. Likewise, as the public's reading tastes matured, ordinary Americans began to recognize *Sister Carrie* for what it is—a ground-breaking masterpiece and an enduring work of art.

Sister Carrie "leaves behind it an unescapable impression of bigness, of epic sweep and dignity," Dreiser's friend H. L. Mencken once wrote.

Declared the novelist Sinclair Lewis in 1930: "Dreiser's great first novel, *Sister Carrie* . . . came to housebound and airless America like a great free Western wind, and to our stuffy domesticity gave us the first fresh air since Mark Twain and [Walt] Whitman."

* * *

Dreiser was nearly thirty-six years old at the time of *Sister Carrie*'s second debut. He lived another thirty-eight years, during which time he wrote seven novels, numerous short stories, some poetry, four long books of autobiography, several plays, and two volumes of philosophical essays. The peak of his career came in 1925 when he wrote *An American Tragedy*. That book, based on a notorious murder case in New York, was hailed by critics as one of the greatest novels of the twentieth century and brought Dreiser the fame and fortune he had long sought.

Like the successful Carrie Meeber, however, Dreiser found that his public triumph in 1925 did not assure him happiness or contentment. He remained instead what he had always been—a complicated, restless, and emotionally troubled man. Haunted by memories of his impoverished youth, he continued to live in fear of being poor, even though he was wealthy enough in the 1920s to rent a fashionable New York apartment and hire servants. He also continued to struggle in his personal relationships. He and Sara never divorced, but they stopped living together after 1914. In 1919, Dreiser began living with another woman, Helen Richardson, whom he finally married in 1944 after Sara's death. But even Helen was not a partner to whom the childless Dreiser could remain faithful, and he drifted in and out of relationships with women throughout his life. Meanwhile, his circle of male friends was small, and he made it even smaller by driving away people with his arrogance and unreasonableness. "Mentally," he said in 1938, "I am as alone as a tramp."

After spending much of his adult life in New York, Dreiser eventually moved to California. It was there, in Hollywood, that he died of a heart attack at age seventy-four on December 28, 1945. Because Dreiser was neither widely loved nor well understood by the American people, the news of his death didn't lead to an outpouring of tributes. In Indiana, people continued to warmly remember Dreiser's brother Paul, who died in 1906 and whose song "On the Banks of the Wabash" became the official state song. But Hoosiers found it harder to recall the younger Dreiser with fondness. They never appreciated the unflattering way he described his home state in his autobiographical works, *A Hoosier Holiday* and *Dawn*. And they were irritated with and embarrassed by his rebelliousness. Why couldn't he, they wondered, have been like them?

Courtesy Vigo County Historical Society

Dreiser in 1908, soon after *Sister Carrie* was republished.

* * *

DETAILS are what made *Sister Carrie* and other Dreiser novels seem so real. As H. L. Mencken, a respected literary critic and a friend of Dreiser's, once noted:

When he described a street in Chicago and New York it was always a street that he knew as intimately as the policeman on the beat, and he never omitted any detail that had stuck in his mind—a queer sign, a shopkeeper standing in his doorway, a leaky fireplug, an ashcan, a stray dog. When he sent some character into an eating-house for a meal it was always some eating-house that he had been to himself, and the meal he described in such relentless detail was one he had eaten, digested and remembered. Coming to the departure or arrival of a train, he commonly gave the precise time, and it could be verified by the railroad schedule. Nearly all the people of his novels were people he had known, man and woman alike . . .

But Dreiser never saw it as his mission to conform. He defined himself as the challenger to conventional thinking, as the truth-teller who sought to provide an accurate picture of life and to see beyond the stereotypes of proper society. He wanted honor and recognition for his work. He wanted to be respected. But as he himself noted in 1923, "Like a kite, I have risen against the wind—not with it."

Though many scholars and historians are quick today to attest to Dreiser's importance in American literature, perhaps the best summation of his enormous influence was offered by his friend H. L. Mencken. Writing after Dreiser's death, Mencken noted:

While Dreiser lived all the literary snobs . . . devoted themselves to reminding him of his defects. He had, to be sure, a number of them . . . But the fact remains that he was a great artist, and that no other American of his generation left so wide and handsome a mark upon the national letters. American writing, before and after his time, differed almost as much as biology before and after Darwin. He was a man of large originality, of profound feeling, and of unshakable courage. All of us who write are better off because he lived, worked and hoped.

SUGGESTIONS FOR FURTHER READING

Dreiser, Theodore. *A Hoosier Holiday*. New York: John Lane Company, 1916.

Dreiser, Theodore. *An Amateur Laborer*. Philadelphia: University of Pennsylvania Press, 1983.

Dreiser, Theodore. *Dawn*. New York: Horace Liveright, Inc., 1931.

Dreiser, Theodore. *Newspaper Days*. Edited by T. D. Nostwich. Philadelphia: University of Pennsylvania Press, 1991.

Lingeman, Richard. *Theodore Dreiser: At the Gates of the City (1871–1907)*. Vol. I. New York: G. P. Putnam's Sons, 1986.

Lingeman, Richard. *Theodore Dreiser: An American Journey (1908–1945)*. Vol. II. New York: G. P. Putnam's Sons, 1990.

Lundquist, James. *Theodore Dreiser*. New York: Frederick Ungar Publishing Company, 1974.

Lydenberg, John, editor. *Dreiser: A Collection of Critical Essays*. Englewood Cliffs, N.J.: Prentice-Hall, Inc., 1971.

Pizer, Donald, editor. *New Essays on Sister Carrie*. Cambridge: Cambridge University Press, 1991.

Sloane, David E. E. *Sister Carrie: Theodore Dreiser's Sociological Tragedy*. New York: Twayne Publishers, 1992.

Swanberg, W. A. *Dreiser*. New York: Charles Scribner's Sons, 1965.

SISTER CARRIE

(FROM CHAPTER IV)

ON MONDAY she arose early and prepared to go to work. She dressed herself in a worn shirtwaist of dotted blue percale, a shirt of light brown serge rather faded, and a small straw hat which she had worn all summer at Columbia City. Her shoes were rather worn at tips and heels, and her necktie was in that crumpled, flattened state which time and much wearing impart. She made a very average-looking shop girl, with the exception of her features. These were slightly more even than is common in women, and gave her a sweet, somewhat reserved air which was pleasing.

It is no easy thing to get up early in the morning when one is used to sleeping until between seven and eight, as Carrie had been at home. She gained some inkling of the character of Hanson's life when, half-asleep, she looked out into the dining room at six o'clock and saw him silently finishing his breakfast. By the time she was dressed he was gone, and she, Minnie, and the baby ate together, the latter being just old enough to sit by in a high chair and disturb the dishes with a spoon. Her spirits were greatly subdued now when the fact of entering upon strange and untried duties confronted her. Only the ashes of all her fine fancies were remaining—ashes still concealing, nevertheless, a few red embers of hope. So subdued was she by her weakening nerves that she ate quite in silence, going over imaginary conceptions of the character of the shoe company, the nature of the work, her employer's attitude. She was vaguely feeling that she should come in contact with the great owners, that her work should be where grave, stylishly-dressed men occasionally look on.

"Well, good luck," said Minnie, when she was ready to go. They had agreed it was best to walk, that morning at least, to see if she could do it every day, sixty cents a week for car fare being quite an item under the circumstances.

"I'll tell you how it goes tonight," said Carrie.

Once in the sunlit street, with laborers tramping by in either direction, the horse cars passing, crowded to the rails with the small clerks and floor help in the great wholesale houses, and men and women generally coming out of doors and passing about the neighborhood, Carrie felt slightly reassured. In the sunshine of the morning beneath the wide blue heavens, with a fresh wind astir, what fears, except the most desperate, can find harborage in the human breast? In the night or the gloomy chambers of the day, fears and misgivings wax strong, but out in the sunlight there is for a time cessation even of the terror of death.

Carrie went strongly forward until she crossed the river and turned into Fifth Avenue. The thoroughfare, in this part, was like a walled canon of brown stone and dark red brick. The big windows of plate glass looked shiny and clean. Trucks were rumbling in increasing numbers; men and women, girls and boys were moving onward in all directions. She met girls her own age who looked at her as if with contempt for her diffidence. She wondered at the magnitude of this life and at the importance of knowing much in order to do anything in it at all. Dread at her own inefficiency crept upon her. She would not know how, she would not be quick enough. Had not all the other places refused her because she did not know something or other? She would be scolded, abused and ignominiously discharged.

It was with but weak knees and a slight catch in her breathing that she came up to the great shoe company at Adams and Fifth Avenue and entered the elevator. When she stepped out on the fourth floor there was no one at hand, only great aisles of boxes piled to the ceiling. She stood, very much frightened, awaiting some one, when a young man with some order slips in his hand got off the elevator.

"Who is it you want?" he asked her.

"Mr. Brown."

"Oh," he said.

Presently Mr. Brown came up. He did not seem to recognize her.

"What is it you want?" he questioned.

Carrie's heart sank.

"You said I should come this morning to see about work—"

"Oh," he interrupted. "Um—yes. What is your name?"

"Carrie Meeber."

"Yes," said he. "You come with me."

He led the way through dark, box-lined aisles which had the smell of new shoes until they came to an iron door which opened into the factory proper. There was a large low-ceiled room with clacking, rattling machines at which men in white shirt sleeves and blue gingham aprons were working. She followed him diffidently through the clattering automatons, keeping her eyes straight before her and flushing slightly. They crossed to a far corner and took an elevator to the sixth floor. Out of the array of machines and benches Mr. Brown signaled a foreman.

"This is the girl," he said, and turning to Carrie, "you go with him." He then returned and Carrie followed her new superior to a little desk in a corner, which he used as a kind of official centre.

"You've never worked at anything like this before, have you?" he questioned rather sternly.

"No sir," she answered.

He seemed rather annoyed at having to bother with such help, but put down her name and then led her across to where a line of girls were sitting on a line of stools in front of a line of clacking machines. On the shoulder of one of the girls who was punching eye holes in one piece of the upper, by the aid of the machine, he put his hand.

"You," he said, "show this girl how to do what you're doing. When you get through, come to me."

The girl so addressed rose promptly and gave Carrie her place.

"It isn't hard to do," she said, bending over. "You just take this so, fasten it with this clamp and start the machine."

She suited action to word, fastened the piece of leather (which was eventually to form the right half of the upper of a man's shoe) by little adjustable clamps, and pushed a small steel rod at the side of the machine. The latter jumped to the task of punching, with sharp, snapping clicks, cutting circular bits of leather out of the side of the upper, leaving the holes which eventually were to hold the laces. After observing a few times, the girl let her work at it alone. Seeing that it was being fairly well done, she went away.

The pieces of leather came from the girl at the machine to her right, and were passed on to the girl at her left. Carrie saw at once that an average speed was necessary or the work would pile up on her and all those below would be delayed. She had no time to look about, and bent anxiously to her task, managing to do fairly well. The girls at her left and right realized her predicament and feelings, and, in a way, tried to aid her as much as they dared by working slower.

At this task she labored incessantly for some time, finding relief from her own nervous fears and imaginings in the humdrum, mechanical movement of the machine. She felt, as the minutes passed, that the room was not very light. It had a thick odor of fresh leather, but that did not worry her. She felt the eyes of the other help upon her and troubled lest she was not working fast enough.

Once when she was fumbling at the little clamp, having made a slight error in setting in the leather, a great hand appeared before her eyes and fastened the clamp for her. It was the foreman. Her heart thumped so that she could scarcely see to go on.

"Start your machine," he said. "Start your machine. Don't keep the line waiting."

This recovered her sufficiently and she went excitedly on, hardly breathing until the shadow moved away from behind her. Then she heaved a great breath.

As the morning wore on the room became hotter. She felt the need of a breath of fresh air and a drink of water but did not venture to stir. The stool she sat on was without a back or footrest and she began to feel uncomfortable. She found after a time that her back was beginning to ache. She twisted and turned from one position to another slightly different, but it did not ease her for long. She was beginning to weary.

"Stand up, why don't you," said the girl at her right, without any form of introduction. "They won't care."

Carrie looked at her gratefully. "I guess I will," she said.

She stood up from her stool and worked that way for awhile, but it was a more difficult position. Her neck and shoulders ached in bending over.

The spirit of the place was one which impressed itself on her in a rough way. She did not venture to look around any, but above the clack of the machines she could hear an occasional remark. She could also note a thing or two out of the side of her eye.

"Did you see Harry last night?" said the girl at her left, addressing her neighbor.

"No."

"You ought to have seen the tie he had on. Gee, but he was a mark."

"S-s-t," said the other girl, bending over her work. The first silenced instantly, assuming a solemn face. The foreman passed slowly along, eyeing each worker distinctly. The moment he was gone, the conversation was resumed again.

"Say," began the girl at her left, "what jeh think he said?"

"I don't know."

"He said he saw us with Eddie Harris at Martin's that night."

"No!" They both giggled.

A youth with tan-colored hair that needed clipping very badly came shuffling along between the machines, bearing a basket of leather findings under his left arm, and pressed against his stomach. When near Carrie he stretched out his right hand and gripped one girl under the arm.

"Aw, let go," she exclaimed angrily—"Duffer."

He only grinned broadly in return.

"Rubber," he called back as she looked after him. There was nothing of the gallant in him.

Carrie got so at last that she could scarcely sit still. Her legs began to tire and she felt as if she would give anything to get up and stretch. Would noon never come? It seemed as if she had worked an entire day already. She was not hungry at all, but weak, and her eyes were tired straining at the one point where the eye-punch came down and clipped the small piece out of the leather. The girl at the right noticed her squirmings and felt sorry for her. She was concentrating herself too thoroughly—what she did really required less mental and physical strain. There was nothing to be done, however. The halves of the uppers came piling steadily down. Her hands began to ache at the wrists and then in the fingers, and toward the last she seemed one mass of dull complaining muscles, fixed in an eternal position and performing a single mechanical movement which became more and more distasteful until at last it was absolutely nauseating. When she was most wondering whether the strain would ever cease, a dull-sounding bell clanged somewhere down an elevator shaft and the end came. In an instant there was a buzz of action and conversation. All the girls instantly left their stools and hurried away into an adjoining room; men passed through, coming from some department which opened on the right. The whirring wheels began to sing in a steadily modifying key until at last they died away in a low buzz. There was an audible stillness in which the common voice sounded strange.

Carrie gladly got up and sought her lunch box. She was stiff, a little dizzy and very thirsty. On the way to the small space portioned off by wood, where all the wraps and lunches were kept, she encountered the foreman, who stared at her hard.

"Well," he said, "did you get along all right?"

"I think so," she replied, very respectfully.

"Um!" he replied, for the want of something better, and walked on.

Under better material conditions this kind of work would not have been so bad, but the new socialism which involves pleasant working conditions for employes had not then taken hold upon manufacturing companies.

The place smelled of the oil of the machines and the new leather—a combination which, added to by the stale odours of the building, was not pleasant even in cold weather. The floor, though regularly swept each evening, presented a littered surface. Not the slightest provision had been made for the comfort of the employes, the idea being that something was gained by giving them as little and making the work as hard and unremunerative as possible. What we know of foot rests, swivel-back chairs, dining rooms for the girls, clean aprons and curling irons supplied free, and a decent cloak room, were unthought of. The wash rooms and lavatories were disagreeable, crude, if not foul places, and the whole atmosphere was one of hard contract.

Carrie looked about her, after she had drunk a tinful of water from a bucket in one corner, for a place to sit and eat. The other girls had ranged themselves about the windows or at the work benches of those of the men who had gone out. She saw no place which did not hold a couple or a group of girls, and being too timid to think of intruding herself and offering friendly overtures, she sought out her machine and, seated upon her stool, opened her lunch on her lap. There she sat, listening to the chatter and comment which went on in different parts of the rooms. It was for the most part silly and graced by the current slang. Several of the men in the room exchanged compliments with the girls at long range.

"Say, Kitty," called one to a girl who was doing a waltz step in a few feet of space near one of the windows—"are you goin' to the ball with me?"

"Look out, Kitty," called another, "you'll jar your back hair."

"Go on, rubber!" was her only comment.

As Carrie listened to this and much more of similar famil-

iar badinage among the men and girls, she instinctively with-
drew into herself. She was not used to this type and felt that
there was something hard and low about it all. She feared that
the young boys about would address such remarks to her—
boys who beside Drouet seemed uncouth and ridiculous. She
made the average feminine distinction between clothes, put-
ting worth, goodness and distinction in a dress suit, and leaving all the unlovely qualities and those beneath notice in overalls and jumper.

She was glad when the short half-hour was over and the
wheels began to whirr again. Though wearied, she would be
inconspicuous. This illusion ended when another young man
passed along the aisle and poked her indifferently in the ribs
with his thumb. She turned about, indignation leaping to her
eyes, but he had gone on and only once turned to grin. She
found it difficult to conquer an inclination to cry.

The girl next her noticed her state of mind.

"Don't you mind," she said. "He's too fresh."

Carrie said nothing but bent over her work. She felt as
though she could hardly endure such a life. Her idea of work
had been so entirely different. All during the long afternoon
she thought of the city outside with its imposing show, crowds
and fine buildings. Columbia City and the better side of her
home life came back. By three o'clock she was sure it must be
six, and by four it seemed as if they had forgotten to note the
hour and were letting all work overtime. The foreman became
a true ogre, prowling constantly about, keeping her tied down
to her miserable task. What she heard of the conversation
about her only made her feel sure that she did not want to
make friends with any of these. When six o'clock came she
hurried eagerly away, her arms aching and her limbs stiff from
sitting in one position.

As she passed out along the hall after getting her hat, a
young machine hand, attracted by her looks, made bold to jest
with her.

"Say, Maggie," he called, "if you'll wait I'll walk with you."

It was thrown so straight in her direction that she knew who was meant but never turned to look.

In the crowded elevator another dusty, toil-stained youth tried to make an impression on her by leering in her face.

One young man, waiting on the walk outside for the appearance of another, grinned at her as she passed.

"Ain't goin' my way, are you?" he called jocosely.

Carrie turned her face to the west with a subdued heart. As she turned the corner she saw through the great shiny window the small desk at which she had applied. There were the crowds hurrying with the same buzz and energy-yielding enthusiasm. She herself felt a slight relief, but it was only at her escape. She felt ashamed in the face of the better-dressed girls who went by. She felt as though she should be better served, and her heart revolted.

THEODORE DREISER interrupted his literary career for long stretches in his later years to follow another powerful urge—namely, an urge to reform America. Beginning in the 1920s, he became involved in a wide range of social issues, from investigating the working conditions of poor coal miners in Kentucky to denouncing the jailing of an anarchist in California. He also became increasingly interested in communism and visited Russia in 1927 to learn more about its political system. For years afterward, Dreiser supported the communist cause in America through his political writings and lectures. Eventually, he joined the Communist party in the United States.

As passionately as he crusaded for social and political reforms, however, he wasn't taken seriously. He was seen by many Americans as lacking common sense and being ruled by his emotions. When he ventured out on the lecture circuit, people attended his talks not so much to hear what he had to say, but to see the man—the tall, homely, awkward Hoosier who relished being the nonconformist. W. A. Swanberg argues, in his biography on Dreiser, that "given any sort of following, [Dreiser] could have been a dangerous man—the emotional visionary."

But, Swanberg continued: "Luckily, a conviction was growing that there was something wrong with him. Yet he would remain for the rest of his life the loudest and strangest literary voice in America."

Dreiser (center) on tour in Russia.

A RELATIVE REMEMBERS DREISER

WHILE Theodore Dreiser was alive, many Hoosiers didn't think much of him or his books, as evidenced in 1934 when the state superintendent of public instruction compiled a list of famous Indiana authors and chose not to include Dreiser's name.

Not surprisingly, Dreiser was annoyed that his work wasn't appreciated in his home state. And as one of his relatives reveals in a colorfully-written memoir, Dreiser's frustration with Hoosiers once led to an outburst in which he refused to return to Indiana for a family reunion.

The relative, Hale T. Shenefield, was a distant cousin of Dreiser's. Shenefield's great-grandmother Susan Schanab and Dreiser's mother Sarah Schanab were sisters. Born in 1902 in Kosciusko County, Indiana, near Warsaw, Shenefield grew up hearing family stories about Theodore and his songwriting brother Paul. But it wasn't until many years later, in 1935, that Shenefield and Dreiser first met. And it wasn't until several decades later, shortly before his death in Virginia in 1981, that Shenefield decided to share his recollections of his famous cousin in an unpublished paper he titled "A Personal Memoir of Theodore Dreiser."

The place of the first meeting between the two men was Toledo, Ohio, where Shenefield worked in county government. Dreiser, who was sixty-four at the time, was scheduled to give a lecture; Shenefield, who had begun reading Dreiser's books while a student at the University of Michigan, decided to attend. After the lecture, Shenefield telephoned Dreiser at his hotel and invited him to lunch. Dreiser accepted, and the two spent a long afternoon together, with the novelist offering opinions on everything from politics to religion.

At one point in the conversation, Shenefield did what his mother had long wanted him to do: he invited Dreiser to return to Indiana for a family reunion, yet to be arranged. As Shenefield's memoir notes, the invitation ignited a reaction in Dreiser—one for which Shenefield was hardly prepared:

With [the invitation] he literally exploded saying, "I won't go back to Indiana—the Editor of the Fort Wayne *Journal Gazette* denounces me as a moral leper—the President of Indiana University disowns me—they've burned my books in Angola—the Warsaw Library where I used to live hasn't a single one of my books—no—I'll never go back there!"

I responded simply and truthfully (though I knew of his general scandal scarred reputation since *Sister Carrie*) that neither I, and certainly not his other relatives, had heard of all these things and in any case they had nothing to do with our appreciation of him and our hope that he might sometime come back for a visit. Thus mollified, we went onto other things.

Soon after that meeting, Dreiser wrote Shenefield from his home in New York. In that letter, Dreiser apologized for his outburst, saying he had mistakenly thought the proposed reunion would be "part of some public procedure—looking to a formal and advertised return . . ." He added that he was "sorry

Courtesy Anne Shenefield Dowd

From the left, Hale T. Shenefield, Norma Bird Shenefield, Dreiser, and Helen in 1937.

that he didn't understand it more fully" and affirmed that a reunion without publicity would be—in Shenefield's words—"a pleasure to him."

The two continued to keep in touch after that, with Dreiser inviting his cousin in 1937 to his New York home called Iroki, which Shenefield remembered as "a queer looking frame and stone house of one and a half stories built as if it were on different levels." In the spring of 1937, Dreiser and Helen Richardson attended Shenefield's wedding in New York City.

Correspondence between the two continued, but the reunion never took place. Dreiser's political views, especially his support for communism and his tolerance of Nazi leader Adolf Hitler, put him far out of step with the American public in the late 1930s and early 1940s. Shenefield, who by then had moved to Washington, D.C., and worked as an economist for the federal government, felt that the timing was not right for inviting Dreiser back to Indiana. "I could hardly have taken responsibility for exhibiting his political positions to his relatives nor would they have received them kindly," he wrote in his memoir.

When Dreiser died in 1945, Shenefield was left with mixed feelings about his complicated cousin. He disagreed with Dreiser's politics, considered Dreiser's treatment of his two wives to be "scandalous," and was skeptical as to whether Dreiser accurately described his boyhood homes ("their houses were not all hovels as Dreiser seems to want readers to believe.")

Even so, there was a side to the novelist that Shenefield liked. "My experience with Dreiser was not extensive," Shenefield recalled, "but it was enough to have experienced his charm . . . when he wanted to be charming."

John Paul Dreiser.   Sarah Schanab Dreiser.

Theodore Dreiser's birthplace in Terre Haute.

Photos courtesy Vigo County Historical Society

(Right) Dreiser's War-
saw home.(Below) A
college freshman,
Dreiser (seated, second
from right in rear)
poses with a cave-
exploring group at
Indiana University.

Sketch by Frederick Booth for *A Hoosier Holiday*

Dreiser as a St. Louis
newspaperman at age
twenty-two.

Dreiser at middle age
with his dog Nick at his
country home near Mt.
Kisco, New York.

Photos courtesy Vigo County Historical Society

The often gloomy Dreiser shown in one of his lighter moods.

INDEX

Note: An asterisk (*) after a number indicates that a photo appears on that page.